GOOD T.A.L.K.
GREAT SALES

Dear Jay,

Thank you so much for your time, talent, and wisdom! It is very much appreciated. I hope you enjoy my book! :)

Sincerely,

"Isaiah: 40:31"

GOOD T.A.L.K. GREAT SALES

The Radically Different Sales
Process and Communication Skills
of Top Producers

ROBERT PAOLINI

GOOD T.A.L.K. GREAT SALES: The Radically Different Sales Process and Communication Skills of Top Producers

Robert Paolini

ISBN: 978-0-578-56392-3

Published by Paolini Properties, Inc.

PRAISE FOR *GOOD T.A.L.K. GREAT SALES*

In an age where there is considerable focus on determining your "why," on becoming a captivating storyteller, and being a solution-based and consultative-oriented sales executive, there is a massive void regarding the how.

Robert Paolini's groundbreaking book combines both impressive research and scholarship along with a remarkable ability to synthesize complex and comprehensive human and career developmental models into crystallized and achievable blueprints for success, which is evident on each page of his book.

Sales professionals who are serious about maximizing their potential will immediately recognize that GOOD T.A.L.K. GREAT SALES will become the equivalent of a five-year head start on taking one's career to the next level.

Gino Blefari, Chief Executive Officer,
Home Services of America, Inc

"It's hard to meet him and not be charmed by his sincerity and energized by his enthusiasm." That is what I said the first time I talked to my wife about this great guy named Bobby that I had just met when he was considering coming to work for us. Our first meeting was more about getting to know each other and comparing values to ensure they aligned. In our conversation, we knew that we looked at so many things similarly, but that does not necessarily mean that working together would be a good fit. There had to be something more substantial in our connection. We found that bond in our desired treatment of the customer.

You see, what makes Bobby unique is simple, yet uncommon. Within one conversation, he can get five things out of it, and all of them are a better way to connect with and represent the customer's best interest. That comes from a passion to achieve—not for himself but to serve his customer. I am proud to have watched his meteoric rise to a level of personal accomplishment that is rarely achieved in business. What's more, he now wants to share his knowledge and approach with other through his new book. Anyone wanting to achieve more in business while honoring others would be wise to read it!

Matt Vigh, Berkshire Hathaway Broker
and Market President

GOOD T.A.L.K. GREAT SALES *maps out a life of purpose for any professional whose values align with biblical principles. It is packed with technical applications that are very effective in today's fast pace of information, data, and technology. The best part is the positive effect it has on the reader professionally and personally. If you are looking to grow yourself and your business, this is a book you are sure to enjoy and come back to time and time again.*

Todd Hopkins, Founder & CEO, Office Pride Commercial Cleaning Services, International best-selling author, *The Stress Less Business Owner*

Robert Paolini's book does a wonderful job of intertwining proven business with life principles and clearly demonstrates these through life experiences. Robert does an elegant job of conveying the concepts and activities that lead to success in business and in life. The book is so compelling and relevant that we plan to provide a copy of GOOD T.A.L.K. GREAT SALES *to every person who joins our team.*

D. Dewey Mitchell and Allen S. Crumbley, Co-Brokers/ Co-Owners, Berkshire Hathaway Home Services Florida Properties Group

I have great admiration for authors whose purpose is to transform the reader from ordinary to extraordinary. In GOOD T.A.L.K. GREAT SALES, *Robert Paolini provides a superlative guide for any impassioned professional wanting to achieve success.*

I have seen speakers and authors as pretenders in this arena, making no mark of real influence. Mr. Paolini is the real deal! Any professional aspiring to be better, who follows the vital principles laid out in his book, will be positively influenced and have a much better chance of achieving greatness in their lives and careers.

Joe Yazbeck, Founder, Prestige Leadership Advisors Bestselling author of *No Fear Speaking*, **speaker, and leadership coach.**

GOOD T.A.L.K. GREAT SALES *is not only an essential read for anyone pursuing a career in sales, it is also a blueprint for how to walk through life as you associate with others. Robert has touched on many relationship building techniques that have been lost over the years. This book is timeless and is a must read for us all!*

Rich Winslow III, Entrepreneur

We all want to surround ourselves with people we know, like, and trust. Communication is essential to learning about others and in turn determining if we like and trust them enough to want to call them a friend or colleague. Beware, communication is a two-way street in which others are also learning about us through our own communication skills so that they too can determine if they want to call us friends, colleagues, or do business with us. In GOOD T.A.L.K. GREAT *SALES, Robert Paolini provides a clear roadmap to success and teaches you how to communicate (and listen) with intention while at the same time keeping your mind focused and heart open. Remember, happiness is a choice and success is the byproduct of a positive attitude. Let Robert Paolini be your tour guide as he leads you on a self-awareness journey towards success.*

Jonathan M. Palma, Esq.
Attorney/Owner, Palma Title and Real Estate Closings

FOREWORD

Trust. It is what's at the heart of every successional relationship, whether it be with customers and prospects, coworkers, friends, or with our family. Trust allows transactions to take place—to know that we can proceed in good faith with another human being. Without this vital element, it is difficult to produce positive outcomes because each party is weary of each other's motives.

Think about it for a moment. Can you recall a bad experience with a salesperson? Most likely, you felt that they simply did not care about you or their presentation was not getting through to you—it was not a match. Now remember a time when you had a positive sales experience. Chances are you were connecting well with the other person, they were speaking your language, meeting your needs, and you felt like you were able to trust them enough to make a purchase.

After you read a few pages of this book, you will quickly realize that the content Robert provides is not your usual sales information about memorizing scripts, closing techniques, handling objections, or identifying benefits. Not that there is anything wrong with learning these things, but this book goes well beyond these basics to the very essence of how to quickly and effectively connect with another human being at a very deep level—the level of trust. It is here where we can more easily influence others and sales are made. *But* this only happens when the person you are speaking to knows that you have their back, and that you are truly there to help solve their problems. Robert distills this process and provides clear direction for accomplishing this.

When you start to communicate with others with this mindset, you will find that you no longer need to use memorized scripts because your focus is now on the other person and solving their problems. You will also notice that you experience fewer objections, and the ones you do receive seem to easily fall away. Sales happen naturally and easily.

Robert also shares the importance of clearifying our own motives and inner game and shares his unique methods for goal setting, eliminating negative talk, and establishing the behaviors that lead to success. This advice shouldn't be taken lightly as Robert has enjoyed a quick and meteoric rise to sales stardom as a top producer in real estate. And now he shares the exact principles, concepts, and motivation that have propelled his career.

Having worked with hundreds of authors and with over thirty years of sales and business experience, I can confidently say this book is a real game changer. Whether you are in sales and want to take your career to the next level, a sales manager looking for a fresh approach for your salespeople, or if you're simply a human being wanting to connect more deeply with others, GOOD T.A.L.K. GREAT SALES is a book that will make a difference in your life and consequently the lives of those you come in contact with.

Howard VanEs, President, Let's Write Books, Inc.

DEDICATION

This book is dedicated to all the real estate and sales professionals who are living the life of results-based income! It's for those who want the best for their clients, friends, family, and community, and it's for those professionals who commit themselves to excellence in serving others.

It is my wish that this world of self-checkout, do it yourself, and automated computers does not replace a handshake's kind nature or the strength of face-to-face communication. May this book help those good people who simply want to help other good people reach their goals with honesty and integrity.

ACKNOWLEDGEMENTS

I would like to acknowledge and express my sincerest gratitude to those who have had a positive impact on writing and finishing this book. I thank my wife, Leika, for your contribution to the editing of the book as well as your loving support to share it with the world. Thank you for allowing me the time to give to its content. I want to also thank our three children (Mia, Ella, and Tripp) for giving me the inspiration and motivation to achieve a goal that is very important to me and our future. In my effort to teach you all the power of believing in your dreams, I have accomplished one of my own.

It has been said that no one accomplishes great things or attains massive success alone, and this book and I are no exception. Thank you to my coach, Joe Yazbeck, for building the dream team around me to create this amazing book, as well as my publisher, Howard VanEs, from Let's Write Books, Inc. Your kind yet honest support turned what started as a proverbial journal of my journey to great success in real estate and sales into an amazing and well-written book.

I also want to acknowledge the owners and brokers (Dewey, Allen, and Matt) of our Berkshire Hathaway office for your support in not only the content and distribution of the book, but also your faith in me and guidance in showing me great ways to better my business and share it with all the agents in the company. Your wisdom and systems helped me to form some of the most successful concepts found in the book.

A special thanks goes to the many authors of all the books I have read over the years that had a major part in my success and also contributed to many of the principles in this book. Finally, I want to thank God for saving my life and guiding me to follow my dream and share what I learned with the world. This book was written sincerely and lovingly for the sole purpose of sharing the proven principles of success. I hope you enjoy reading it as much as I did writing it.

TABLE OF CONTENTS

INTRODUCTION

The information in this book solves enormous problems for salespeople. What problems, you may be asking? If you've wondered whether you can survive or thrive in a shifting or depreciating market, read on. Or, if you have asked yourself any of the next four questions, this book was written for you.

Those questions are:

1. How can I avoid the income roller coaster effect of results-based sales?
2. How can I get predictable results in my market?
3. How can I build and sustain quality business relationships?
4. How can I be more productive and convert more opportunities into great sales?

The book has two main purposes. One is to educate through a uniform vision of a culture, methodology, and physical process for great success in any type of sales job. Your goal is to learn the principles and practices of success in business, as well as relationship building and cultivation. The other purpose is to help improve your life from the inside out so that you can do, be, or have more, and so you're not only able to handle a wider array of problems, but welcome them as ways to grow. You will find that these principles can very much make you a better parent, a better spouse, a better friend, and better to yourself.

Finally, this book was written to teach work/life balance and good daily habits that produce greater results no matter the field. Consistent rituals are the most underrated practice for success. People always underestimate what they can do within a day and overestimate what they can accomplish in ten years. *Good T.A.L.K. Great Sales* will guide you through a process of creating a new mindset and provide examples of daily habits and rituals to develop the necessary discipline for growth as well as specific communication techniques that bring consistent positive results.

In a world where most people would rather just hear a two-minute joke, laugh, and be done with it, there are people out there who take great pride in seeing others succeed, and get value from sharing that wisdom, which is my purpose here. But what you'll get from this book is far more than you could ever get from any joke—it'll add so much more value to your life than any bit of entertainment, sporting event, or concert.

You could Google what to do next in your life to be successful, or even what not to do. But the main principle of this book is that you must do things consistently. Without an effective, positive, and powerful mindset, you won't even understand why you should do, or—at the very least—keep doing those daily actions which take physical discipline. Therefore, if you can't do that, you actually won't achieve your goals because you won't be doing the physical practices of your occupation that bring in money. It is a slow process, but I guarantee that if you follow what is presented in this book, you can achieve success.

The title *Good T.A.L.K. Great Sales* is exceedingly important to understanding the context of the principles inside this book. To begin, "good" means the opposite of bad or evil. It's also a way of being, or a state of mind, like an intention (good intentions). Trying to be good and evil would be like trying to go somewhere by slamming the brakes and the gas at the same time. "T.A.L.K." is an acronym for the four pillars of communication that are most important when communicating. You could use them with your children, your spouse, a neighbor, a friend, a co-worker, boss, client, colleague, or lead. These pillars establish the framework for effective verbal communication. We are surrounded by so many communication platforms built with technology, like social media, that we are becoming less social.

"T" stands for "truth" as well as "tonality." Being truthful—telling, speaking, and thinking the truth is first and foremost. Truth comes even before love, happiness, and health. Because if everything around us is a lie, and the things that people are saying to us and we're saying to them are not true, then nothing really matters.

It is also important to be truthful to ourselves. If you are still questioning love and truth, remember that you can always have truth without love, but you cannot have love without truth. For example, I love my wife dearly for many reasons. However, those reasons are all based on the truths of her that I hold in my mind. These truths define her to me, and the world around me. If my feelings are based on that truth, the moment that truth becomes a lie, the feelings are invalidated. However, there are plenty of people I trust that

I don't love. Tonality is important because if you're just texting something, you could say the same sentence—an eight-word sentence—eight different ways. For example:

"*I* didn't stub my toe on the bed."
"I *didn't* stub my toe on the bed."
"I didn't *stub* my toe on the bed."
"I didn't stub *my* toe on the bed."
"I didn't stub my *toe* on the bed."
"I didn't stub my toe *on* the bed."
"I didn't stub my toe on *the* bed."
"I didn't stub my toe on the *bed*."

See what I mean? Emphasizing the different words changes the meaning every time. There is another principle that says 55 percent of communication comes from the body language of the other person, including their physical appearance. It also says that 38 percent of communication comes from the tone or tempo the other person is using when they are speaking, and 7 percent comes from the actual words the person is using. Simply knowing that could make all the difference for you!

The "A" is "attention." Attention has become the greatest commodity on Earth, and companies spend billions of dollars to get it. You're using it right now to understand these words. If we were sitting across from each other at a table, and I were looking away while you were talking, that would seriously affect our communication. Social media, however, only works because people want attention. They want your eyes and ears, so they can sell us what they are producing. Big companies also crave your attention so that you ignore their competitors. All of that stuff works because they know how our minds work and how we perceive things. That being said, a decision is no longer required to make a sale, just our attention, and that leaves the door open to plant the seeds in our minds so that we sell it to ourselves and not even know it. Take Coca Cola, for example, a massive company that is so good at getting our attention that they have built a culture that simply requires a reminder for a call to action because they are already branded in our minds. What they are selling is "carbonated sugar water" if you think about it, but we won't because Coca Cola defines it for us. If we gain the attention of the prospective client, we can cut through the noise around them and create an open channel direct to them, allowing us to ask them to do and buy with ease. Therefore, giving and receiving attention is valuable. Use it more than you are used by it. Pay attention!

The "L" stands for "listening," which is the verb form of what attention really is. It's the proactive form of attention. Listening, especially listening first, is the same as seeking to understand before trying to be understood. It means listening to every word with the goal to learn something, perhaps change or alter a perspective which may very well be your own. If there are two sides to a given conversation, we must aim to understand both to truly understand the big picture.

It is through that process that a solution can be found. Most people listen with the intent to speak; they are just waiting on their turn. Others believe that letting the other person speak is just common courtesy. It may appear that way, but that is just a bonus. The real value of listening is to gather information that can be used to help your client. It also drops the guard of the other person, and if this is an adversary, you want all the leverage you can get. If you can do that while making the other person think they are in control, all the better. It also goes without saying that if neither person in a conversation is listening to the other, they are not actually communicating. They are just making noise. It is in the perception and conception of another from another that actually defines communication. Whether it's in negotiations, a lecture, or you're just trying to read the feelings of somebody you care about—listening is absolutely paramount.

The "K" stands for "kindness." Kindness is the attitude which we should all have when communicating. So whether you're having a bad day or not liking the person you're talking to at the moment, you still should always be kind. We all are defined by the way we treat ourselves and others. You've must understand that we're all in the same fight. Solving a problem is only going to be accomplished through proper communication, and you must have compassion and kindness to do so successfully. That way, you can see the big picture and not have your feelings influence you, be it through jealousy, frustration, or something else. For instance, if you're scared or worried, those kinds of feelings will inhibit your ability to listen and understand.

Similarly, if you are angry or you dislike the other person, you will have your thoughts clouded and won't have the capacity to find a unified solution to the problem or answer to a question. Your own negative emotions may also alter the other person's thinking not allowing them to understand you which could increase your frustration. If you're not feeling happy being kind, your facial expressions and body language will also be affected. As mentioned, body language and physical appearance are 55 percent of communication between two people. If you have not closed a deal, or aren't connecting with your client and have no idea why, it might be because you are not communicating on this level as this is the foundation of trust and rapport.

However, if you have a kind tone, welcoming body language, and a smile on your face, then the communication will be much better. In real estate, this is a proven fact. I might be battling prices on contracts, or critical tasks during inspection periods. It's really just all about being kind and turning the other person into your client's advocate. If the other side likes you, you will be surprised by what they are willing to do, or willing to concede for you or your client, but if they don't, you won't like what they are willing to do just to throw the whole deal away. Simply put, always use kindness, respect, and compassion when communicating.

Good T.A.L.K Great Sales covers (what I call) the four pillars of communication. As you read this book, you are going to develop a better understanding of this information as you dive deeper into common principles of general communication, and then to more specific applications in relationship building, relationship cultivation, networking, and perfecting the network effect for almost any type of sales position or industry that requires you to acquire your own clients.

Communication is vital for making the sale, so as long as we are being 100 percent honest with ourselves and others, using a professional and positive tone, paying close attention to the other person and listening very intently to learn, find solutions, and convey understanding to the other party. We can most certainly turn a good T.A.L.K. into great sales!

BONUS FOR READERS OF *GOOD T.A.L.K. GREAT SALES*

Ten productivixty hacks for salespeople. Get it done quicker, better, easier!

Download it here: **https://goodtalknation.com/bonus**

HA.
HE.
WI.
WE.

A Good T.A.L.K. Begins with Understanding How to Think

If we are to attain great wealth, we must learn how to effectively communicate to one another, but to do that we must be mindful of our thoughts, emotions, and how we communicate to ourselves. That is what HA.HE. WI.WE. is all about. It is the temporal order of thought and emotionally successive state of consciousness. In other words, what do we need to know, and in what order of importance, to keep our minds, bodies, and attitudes in

Tree of life (Ha, He, Wi, We)

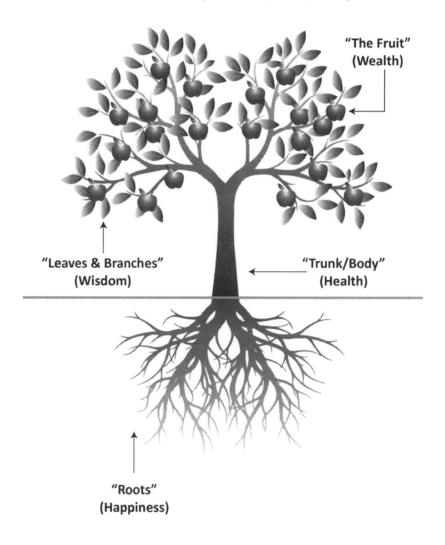

"The Fruit" (Wealth)

"Leaves & Branches" (Wisdom)

"Trunk/Body" (Health)

"Roots" (Happiness)

a balanced state for good? You could also think of it as a mnemonic mantra (MM) that will guide your day and shape your life. To compare HA.HE. WI.WE. to something familiar, it would be similar to Hakuna Matata from Disney's *The Lion King*. Think of it as a fun chant to anchor in that MM to create a subconscious effect in our minds to create habits.

The best part about HA.HE.WI.WE. is that it can be proven over time by putting it into action. It can also be found in nature. (See illustration of the *tree of life*). *Seeing* how HA.HE.WI.WE. works in this example will help you better understand its meaning to you. As you can see from the illustration below, the roots of the tree are like our minds and emotions where our happiness dwells. The trunk of the tree is like our physical bodies as a conduit between the roots and the fruits, similar to our own consciousness and our reality. The branches and leaves collect the resources required to create the fruit, much the same way we learn and gain knowledge (wisdom). The fruit of the tree is the gift for all to share, similar to the way we would create wealth or success toward a purpose by thinking positive thoughts, taking care of our bodies, and increasing our knowledge to have a greater impact on the world around us (sharing our fruit).

Now that you understand what it means, you are probably wondering what it stands for! HA.HE.WI.WE. includes the first two letters of happy, healthy, wise, and wealthy. Now that I have your attention, let me explain.

HAPPY

It's no coincidence that happy is first on the list! In fact, all these items complete a successive, never-ending loop. The first fact you must anchor into your mind is that happiness (in this case) is not an effect, or a reaction, nor is it dependent on external factors. Happiness is a choice. It is quite literally an emotional state of mind that is entirely your choice. It has also been called our true freedom. You see, liberty is gained by our own agreement with one another that if you play by the rules, you are free to live as you are. Freedom, however, is our ability to control how we feel no matter the situation. As Steven Covey says in his book, *7 Habits of Highly Effective People*, between what happens to us (a stimulus or event or action toward us) and how we react to it, there is a space, and within that space is our freedom to choose how we will feel about that stimulus. In other words, we may allow past events, emotional or physical, to determine the way we look at things, or even allow them to determine how they make us feel, but the reality is that we do not have to, nor should we.

It is first on the list because you cannot effectively flow through the other states of mind (HA.HE.WI.WE.) without it. Think about how you feel and the way you look at things when you are angry or sad. Willpower plummets, energy levels drop, and your attitude originates from a more negative perspective. If we do not start each and every day truly happy, the rest of the day will most likely be swayed by anything that comes your way, good or bad, and it will create a more reactive, negative, and time-sensitive lifestyle. Most people assume that they have no control over their happiness, so they don't focus on their own state of mind and react to things based on their current emotion. However, if you are starting your day happily, you are then driven by your principles and values. So when something negative happens, you are more capable of solving the problem without allowing it to shift your mental focus.

Our state of mind is not always in the same place each morning. Many things influence it, including our thoughts before we go to bed. For that reason, it is important to make a conscious effort to bring our emotions to a positive state. It will seem like you are faking it at first (because you are) but, before you know it, you truly either wake up happy every day, or it takes nothing more than a few trigger words, or a couple of deep breaths, and you are back in happy mode with a sincerely positive mental attitude. That is truly the beginning because most people have every intention of being happy, but if they are not aware of this fact, then the slightest thing can throw them off. It can happen every day, which would completely prevent that person from sustaining happiness. Negative things will always be a part of life; if we can't avoid them, then we should know how to handle them. At any point, we're all either coming out of a problem, headed toward a problem, or in the middle of a problem, and regardless of the difficulty, remember these four amazing words "this too shall pass." Sometimes there is nothing to be happy about, but that is why God only asks us to have faith. Faith is the root of happiness, and even when all seems lost, we are saved by grace. Even if you won the lottery, you would still have a bad day now and again, and now you know how to handle it. Staying in a controlled, low-level state of happiness through-out the day is the key to massive growth and effectiveness in every aspect of life.

HEALTHY

Once you have made a personal commitment to be happy, you will start your day thinking more about what is good in your life. Gratitude becomes the attitude of choice and is the easiest way to turn a negative emotion into pure joy. Now that we have established the importance of sustaining a happy state of mind, we move on to the next part of HA.HE.WI.WE., the "HE," or healthy. Think back to all the times you may have had a bad cold or flu. Were your thoughts and attitude truly driven around your goals, positive actions, your career, or even having fun? Probably not; all we want when we are sick is to feel better. It greatly affects our will and our ambitions.

In most cases, our energy and mental capacity are also negatively affected. Being sick has a physical tax on our bodies. Those effects (if repeated often enough) could also have a negative influence on our mental state. Having a clouded mind and a weakened body will stop even the most motivated person. If our goals are to thrive, grow, and succeed as we wish, it is easier when we are healthy. That being said, it is our responsibility to take care of our mind, body, and spirit, so that we can maintain our health and be more available as a resource to our clients, friends, and family.

We must do what we can to stay healthy—because we are either overripe and rotting or green and growing. Exercise, as well as good food in mod-eration, is necessary to maintain the physical health and performance of our body. And daily reading, meditation, and prayer is a great way to maintain a low-level positive mental state all the time. It allows us to channel more of our core values so that we are less reactive to things that may surprise us or negative situations we may not yet understand. A healthy body is also the best way to sustain a happy state of mind. For any of these healthy actions, the key is consistency. Making them an everyday habit is the most important part. The important part to remember about health is that it is also a choice, so every day, first make sure you are happy, then make sure you eat well, exercise, get plenty of sleep, and read something that will make you better every day.

WISE

Once we have our attitudes in check by choosing to be happy every day, and we take certain measures to maintain our health, we must then go on a journey to gain wisdom. In HA.HE.WI.WE., the WI stands for wisdom. It's the third step in the path to a balanced mindset. I believe it is our human responsibility to gain wisdom or a skill that we can use to serve others. The next step would be to find what we love and what we are good at and aim to attain mastery in that field as a tree produces fruit to share. As Zig Ziglar said, "When we help enough people get what they want, we will get what we want." So, if we do not have wisdom gained, we don't have anything to give. When we give more than we have, we get tired. When fill ourselves to our capacity, then we begin to overflow into others. When we give more to others than we can hold, it gives us energy rather than taking it away. The goal is to fill your cup until it overflows and then share that excess with others. No matter what field you are in, if part of that job is solving a problem for another, we know what our value is, and we can help others through their own obstacles. That is the key to building and sustaining professional relationships.

If you are reading this and do not know what your value is and what makes you different and better than your competition, the next step would be to sit down as soon as possible and think about all the attributes, qualities, and expertise you have to offer your client. You want to write them all down and think of as many as you can. Gary Keller of Keller Williams says, "A professional is someone who knows what they know, knows what they don't, and knows the difference between the two. So, if you ask a question of a professional and he or she knows the answer, they will tell you, and if they don't, they will find the person with the right answer, so you know you will always get the information you need and the results you want." On a side note, the level of wisdom one has in a particular field is directly connected to the professional confidence level as well. In my world, agents fear calling prospects and hearing something they don't understand or don't have an answer for. Most agents are not familiar enough with a real estate contract to explain it to a seller or buyer, but I can tell you from experience that nothing gives you more confidence than knowing what every word of the contract means. For that reason, my team and I read through the contracts weekly. Be wise.

Whether you are thinking about going back to school for a better career, or going to a trade school for a better job, or learning how to write a book about good communication to help others, you must gain wisdom. Like the branches from the tree of life, we dwell in happy soil, we take care of our body to form a healthy trunk, and we gain the wisdom we need to stretch ourselves like the branches of a tree and share more with others. Our fruit then becomes a seed to the receiver and the process begins again as the next person plants our seed in their soil, taking our wisdom (or good deed) and eventually passing it on to another. Intentional wisdom sets the stage for maximum effectiveness at work and maximum quality time at home, family, and personal relationships. Later, I will show you exactly how to do this. Now that we are happy, healthy, and full of wisdom, we are in a position to receive wealth.

WEALTHY

Finally, we have wealth! Wealth is a subjective term. I always say that gold and God are not at the end of the same path. Furthermore, wealth does not necessarily mean gold and money. Some would say that wealth is nothing more than having choices, and others may say that it is nothing more than a combination of time and money as a resource. To me, wealth is the successful completion of an individual's efforts. For example, I am a realtor, but I am a husband and father first. However, I cannot provide for my family unless I help others complete a real estate goal or solve a real estate problem. Therefore, my wealth would directly result in me being able to come home at an hour that allows for quality time with my wife and children before they go to bed. Whether we talk about what they did that day, or watch a good movie and eat some popcorn, the goal is to be able to enjoy that time with them without worrying. This is also another step toward ensuring happiness. When we are present, we are happy. In other words, we want to ensure that when we are with our family or friends, our minds are too.

Additionally, when we are at work, only keep our clients in our heads, not our family or friends. This will help your memory and keep those endorphins going, and it will put a smile on your face. You see, everything about HA.HE.WI.WE. is connected. One helps the other, and they work in cycles.

So when granted wealth of any size or type, we are motivated to continue moving forward with those small victories. And the cycle continues again with happiness, and then health, which gives us the energy to attain wisdom, which allows us to help more people more effectively, and that grants more wealth. When that process gets repeated over and over, what grows from that is our "why,"—and why we do something is the number one reason we do anything. In the next chapter, we will talk about "The Big Why" and why it is so important!

THE
BIG
WHY

Start Each Day Knowing Why You're Getting Up

The key is doing something because you should, not because you have to. You're aiming to serve people. You're aiming to get things done and achieve your goals. As in Chapter 1, you're starting with happiness, and your health is second most important. Your aim now is to gain wisdom and receive wealth—the goal that is most important to you.

You have to know your *big why*. To better explain the power of the "why," I'll give you a little anecdote. Imagine a two-by-four that's twenty feet long and lying on the floor in your living room. What if I were to ask, "For a hundred bucks, would you walk across that two-by-four?"

Most everyone would say, "Yes. Absolutely, I'll take that hundred bucks and I'll walk across this two-by-four." No big deal. Even if you fall off, who really cares; you're an inch and half off the ground. Well, what if I were to raise that two-by-four to the top of two one-hundred-foot buildings that were about seventeen feet apart, and then I offered you the same hundred dollars to walk across the same two-by-four? Most likely, your answer is going to be no. At this point, you've had no further training, no expertise, no hypnosis, no anything. There's no safety equipment—nothing added. But now, check out this new scenario:

Visualize yourself about to walk across that two-by-four, but the other building is on fire. Let's say that there's a person on the other side and they mean the world to you, like a child or spouse. Would anyone still need a hundred dollars? Absolutely not. You are going to run across that thing, save your child or spouse, and run back.

You've got no extra training, no safety gear. Nothing has changed in this scenario except your big why. Something that was seemingly impossible was done solely because your reason for doing it had intensified. Your why became more vital. Why we do something is the most important factor in getting it done—even if it's why we wake up and do certain morning rituals or things to make our days run better.

Two pillars control your why: belief and value. These both fall under the umbrella of the big why.

Simon Sinek, bestselling author and speaker of one of the most popular TED talks of all time, has said, "People don't buy what you do; they buy why you do it."

This is another good reason to have a why. By leading with your why, your passion, truth, and integrity will be out there for people to see. It's the integrity of the transaction—your big why. If you're selling something that you don't believe in that's going to be obvious, too. Know your big why. Know why you're doing what you do over anything else.

And is it really what you want to do? Maybe that's the problem. Maybe what you're doing isn't satisfying your big why. That's a good reason to double-check yourself and possibly look into a different career. But if you know your big why and that the career you're in can satisfy it, and you start your day happy, healthy, wise, and wealthy—well, my friends, there's nothing in this world that you can't be, do, have, or overcome.

Another way to look at the power of why is by how strongly your body responds to what you are doing. The way that we experience things means more to us than random information. In other words, information learned under pressure, or in a way that can be experienced through our senses, is the strongest way our mind and body define them. Please, allow me to explain.

A Taste of Honey

This story is about perception. Let's say you have never tasted honey. You've heard tantalizing information about it, but you simply lived in a place where you could never obtain it.

When you got out of high school, you went to college and studied everything there was to know about honey. You got your master's in honey. Then, after you did your senior thesis statement about honey, you turned the bee population crisis around and invented foundations for flowers. The accomplishments! You've changed the honey world as we know it—the distribution, the international restrictions, and constraints. Now you're a raw honey advocate in local communities, even pushing it through stores.

You are the master of honey, yet you've never tasted it. But you know everything about it: how it's made, how it's created, the different kinds, the different ways to produce and store it, all about the honeycomb. And because of your crazy amounts of knowledge, because of that information that you've gained by reading books and educating yourself in our traditional education

17

system, you have an identity of honey. Your brain has an opinion of it. It has its own definition of what it is and what it means.

But if you were to taste honey at this point, nothing of what you have learned will matter anymore. The receptors in your brain that define honey will be wiped clean. They will instantly take a backseat to your conscious interpretation of honey. Now you've put it in your mouth. Now your brain has to justify what you just ate, leverage again what it already knows about honey, and give it a new definition. That stimulus is going to create another stimulus. It's going to create a habit.

That habit will be based on sugar, which means you're going to want to eat more honey. The more honey you eat, the more your conscious brain reprograms the subconscious about what honey is and means, as well as its value and purpose. Everything about this sweet, sticky substance is now changing in your mind. You spent the last ten years studying honey—learning everything you could. In just a few days, that's all dissolved—much like a spoonful of honey.

It is a real thing to me—and slightly different from what Webster's Dictionary says. In this example, "consciousness" is any time you are observing things around you using any or all of the five senses. So, a conscious mind is using sight, sound, taste, touch, and smell to identify the world. When you're using any of those senses, you are in a conscious state of mind. If you have a thought in your mind, whatever it is—good, bad, ugly, or scary—but you are not using any of those five senses, you are actually in a subconscious state. You are in what's called deep thought. At this time, you're really thinking about something that's concerning you or that you're trying to define or create a value or a judgment on. Typically, that doesn't make you feel good, right?

When you're using the five senses, you're only absorbing the information around you. So, unless something tastes bad, looks ugly, smells awful, feels weird, or sounds terrible, you're going to be happy. It's the subconscious that usually allows bad feelings to flood in because you're either focusing on future expectations that make you apprehensive, which is where fear comes from, or you're dwelling on the past, which either makes you sad or brings back bad memories, which is where guilt comes from.

By reading this book repeatedly, internalizing and repeating positive affirmations, and establishing good habits for yourself, you are, in essence, retraining your mind to view and define things differently. Or in this case, the way you want, but it must be done daily. That's the best way to make progress—you have to start somewhere. If you want quality results in anything you do, how do you get started? With belief in yourself and the one thing that will prevent you from quitting—your *big why!*

GOALS

The Habit of Getting What You Want

When it comes to goals, it's important to see them as "the habit of getting what you want," or—at the very least—always heading in the right direction. Much like the typical New Year's resolutions, we set them and perhaps even write them down, but we never look at them again. Common practice does not always use common sense. You focus each day around the idea of your long-term goals, yearly goals, quarterly goals, monthly goals, weekly, and daily goals. Goals should be the compass that guides us, keeps us on track, and allows for a better pace. Without that compass, we are most likely operating like a ship lost at sea. It is best described by this famous quote by Lucius Annaeus Seneca: "If one does not know to which port one is sailing, no wind is favorable." Now that you know the power of setting goals, how do we stick to them?

Anchors Away

The best way to stay on course (even if reading your goals every minute is not enough) is to use "anchors," which I will elaborate on shortly. Even the best, most-recited goals are no match for the unknowns of life. Anchors work as a secondary line of defense to prevent you from failing to reach your goals. An anchor, as I will use it in this next example, is a task (usually unfavorable) that is repeated everyday. It's easy to do, but also easy not to do. However, the action should be good for you, but cause a little discomfort or pain.

An easy example of how to see an anchor works is this: Let's say you want to save $12,000 this year for emergencies. It would be logical to save $1,000 every month starting January, and by the end of the year, you will have $12,000. You can look at your current budget to confirm whether this is possible. To help with this, you can also implement a secondary plan to save money in other areas by evaluating what you are spending money on and refine it to what you actually need. That may sound great, but nothing can help you if something unexpected happens, financially or personally. In fact, the first thing that would go if that happens, would be the plan to save $12,000. If this happens to you, you may not be able to save the $1,000 that month, but maybe you can make it up next month. However, things happen, and if the next month is the same, you may find yourself in a position that you can't come back from, and in the end, you may not save anything.

Anchors remind you of your goals. The more difficult/healthy your anchor is, the more important the goal itself becomes to you. If I want to save $12,000 this year, (and I begin exactly how I previously explained), I must be able to overcome difficult situations, and the anchor helps. Let's take running, for example, which is easy to do and easy not to do. It does not take any special training, it is healthy for you, and it is difficult to do for long distances. You must make a personal commitment to the task and the goal (saving $12,000), which is called the "lag goal" or the "end game." Saving $1,000 a month is known as the "lead goal," or the short-term task that leads to the big goal. The reason we call the third part of this goal-setting style an "anchor" is because it anchors your lead goal to your daily consciousness, which embeds it into your subconscious, thereby strengthening your belief in both the lead measure and the lag goals each month. This happens without us realizing it, but it is always working and always expanding. So, for me, I run every morning to primarily remind my body, mind, and spirit that I am committed to my goals and I will not stop running until I hit them. Once that belief becomes permanent, you have made it, and it's only a matter of time until you hit that *big goal*.

Anchors at Depth

There's a much deeper principle about goals and goal setting that you may not even have realized until now. You see, our normal human condition is to be safe, search for comfort, and conserve resources. Therefore, most people wake up and just go through the motions of life, following orders, impulses, and bad habits. The truth is we are always looking for familiar comforts because we don't want to wait for our goals, but we don't want to be miserable either. We end up looking for validation outwardly, judging that information inwardly, and then developing inhibiting beliefs that keep us in a parasympathetic state of mind, which can create chronic negative feelings.

The primary purpose of a goal is to close the gap between where you are and where you want to be—and to also distract you from the impulsive world around you. Setting goals and sticking with your lead measures also makes it possible to be in a positive state of mind even when you do not already have or can see what it is you want. The good news is that progressing toward a goal gives us true happiness along the way. We all have to start somewhere, so if you are thinking you will never be happy until you hit your goal, you may never be happy or hit your goals.

When we learn to set and achieve goals properly, we begin to create the world that we want and not react to a world that is out of our control, which is unlike how most people look at goals. When we focus on what we want, we align it with a definite purpose (formed by the anchor), dwell on the feeling of achievement and its benefits, enjoy the feeling of already achieving the goal mentally, elevate our thoughts to be more positive, and begin to align our actions with our lead and lag goals. Thus, the dreams and goals in our minds we will soon be held in our hands. So, don't allow your thoughts to cause your actions to control you mind and leave you trapped in a world you don't want. Make your mind capable of controlling your actions using goals with the self-discipline using anchors daily, and you will live the life you want and be in full control of your emotions, which is your true, God-given freedom.

Not Just Setting Goals, Achieving Goals

Many people have a myriad of ideas about what it takes to accomplish goals. If you skip a step, you'll never reach the goal. So many people have ideas for goals, but they never achieve them because they're missing the recipe. If I give you all the stuff to make a cake, you still have to know the recipe to follow, and it has to be duplicatable. It's the same reason the gym is always filled with people the first few months of the year. They're missing this next part. Pay close attention to this. It will help you understand the power of goals but also make goal-setting more effective and powerful in your life.

Another example uttered by someone: "The way to success and achieving your goals is to focus." Sounds great, right? In fact, it's cute and fluffy. It's like, "Yeah! I just need to focus!"

But you're skipping so many steps. How do you focus? When? If you are worried about your happiness, and you're miserable and have a bad attitude, or you're in bad shape and you're not eating right, you're going to be very unfocused. Therefore, you won't achieve your goals. Again, it's not just focus. However, it does start with the happy, healthy, wise, and wealthy—in other words, your mindset. This also includes knowing your big why and identifying it every day. I call it visualization. Visualizations are part of a morning ritual which we'll be talking further about—they allow you to see your big why more clearly. Your mindset is the first thing you need to build and expand to achieve your goals.

We are Creatures of Habit

Again, habits taught in this book are not to be done once or twice. Everything must be done daily. We, as humans, are creatures of habit. Therefore, success is not achieved by a single act but through daily practice. Nothing is attained spontaneously because everything is built exponentially. Anything great, anything marvelous—say, an Olympian doing a triple backflip—did not happen because he or she was bold enough to throw themselves into it. It takes thousands upon thousands of hours of mindset, discipline, habits, and brutal, unrelenting practice. Then those things are all wrapped nicely around the other two core principles we talked about in Chapter 2, value and belief. If you don't think what you're doing is going to add value to that big why, you won't do it. Even if you do think a task adds value to your important goal, but you don't believe you can do it, then you won't do it.

For example, before this year, I had not run a mile since high school. I was also told as a freshman that I had a heart murmur. I assumed, in my own mind, that the heart murmur would just linger with me forever and make me feel tired when I ran. So, when I would run for a long distance, I would feel tired and think, "Well, that's because of my heart murmur." Little did I know that everybody feels tired when they run a mile. Newsflash! My inhibiting belief was thinking that my heart murmur was limiting me. So, mindset is the biggest consideration for achieving your goals. You must be aware of the value it adds to you and your goals, and you have to believe in yourself that you can do it.

How Disciplined Habitual Actions Create Exponential Growth

Once you have the mindset and you know that you're on the right path, you must start with a discipline, which in this scenario, means doing something every day whether you want to or not. Decide what consistent actions need to be done to give you the results you truly want based on the results you're not presently receiving. Apply that discipline and know that you're going to do things every single day that you don't want to, just like when we were kids. But living outside that comfort zone will make you better and able to achieve things you normally couldn't. As you do, the next little thing that you couldn't formerly do will lead to doing an even greater thing. Sooner or later, you're going to be able to accomplish things that people cannot believe. When I watch a skier do fifteen flips in the air, it blows my mind. But I didn't see the previous ten thousand hours of practicing one flip, a double flip, a triple flip, and a quad flip. The body just becomes better by mastering one little discipline after another.

Here's the good news: you don't have to apply discipline forever. People always assume that any hardship experienced will linger into the future, that they're always going to hate doing it, that it's always going to be difficult. However, after repetitive actions become habits, powered by discipline, then less discipline is required. It might seem that those habits are becoming a little easier, but really, we are just getting better. In fact, there will always be a chip on your shoulder or there will always be some level of difficulty. I tell my eleven-year-old that there's pressure involved, but you have to understand that it's there and embrace it. You're going to school to learn something you don't know already. That takes effort. It takes mental and physical strength. We seem to get out of school and then abandon that principle, but that's the foundation of exponential growth, whether physical or mental. You've constantly got to be trying to educate yourself about something you don't already know. This is the "WI." in the HA.HE.WI.WE. It's gaining wisdom.

Practice Creates Habits

So, practice those disciplines whether you like it or not, every single day. I always tell myself, "I hope I don't want to do it." It's in those situations that I know I'm going to force myself to do it. I don't care if I've broken my leg or I'm hurting, I'm going to get down to it. That way, my subconscious body won't make excuses for me, like—oh my gosh—my Achilles is hurting, or my knee is strained or sprained, or I'm cramping up—maybe I shouldn't run today. If you let that kind of thinking seep in, it will win, and you'll accomplish nothing. But if you commit to doing something, come hell or high water, no matter how you're feeling—well, I promise you those feelings of pain and destruction won't surface. Because the last thing you're going to want to do is to engage in those disciplines knowing, full well, that you're not 100 percent.

The key to following a discipline is that, at some point, whether it be twenty days, ninety days, or a year—those disciplines will eventually become habits. They will not be as difficult, mentally or physically, yet they will produce better results over and over again. Forming these habits is how you produce amazing results and achieve your goals. Executing good, daily habits gives you consistent results that will achieve any goal you want to accomplish.

It doesn't matter what it is—a new career, getting a raise or promotion, or shifting gears in the industry—the economics in your world around you are shifting, and you need to find other ways to generate income. All of those start from a positive mindset, then the habits come, and they are all wrapped nicely around the value added to your big why and the affirmations that you give yourself every day—the affirmations that say you believe without a doubt, in your heart of hearts, that you can do it.

DAILY
DISCIPLINES

Notice the pattern here. We're starting with the inner and moving up in priority toward the outer. You have to start with things like the mindset, attitude, and the big why, but now we're starting to get into physical tasks, which is the daily discipline. It doesn't matter what you do or want to do for a living. Whether you're training to be a registered nurse, heart surgeon, real estate agent, or a medical salesperson—we're still in principle mode. These are core values and actions that can propel you into stratospheric success in what you're doing.

Now, I'm just the distributor of the following acronym. It actually came from a man named Hal Elrod who wrote *The Miracle Morning*. He calls these daily disciplines "S.A.V.E.R.S." Frankly, this has absolutely "saved" my life. I was looking for something that I could not just know or learn, but actually do. Something that would force to be more productive. I've now reread it many times. The S.A.V.E.R.S. morning rituals are by far the best I've read about and applied, and I want to share them here with you.

A Solid Start to Each Day

S.A.V.E.R.S. is an easy way to remember your daily disciplines. Now, when I was first doing it, I wrote on a sheet of paper for five days a week, "S-A-V-E-R-S," so I'd remember to do everything. Again, as I mentioned in the previous chapter, discipline is only needed in the beginning. As of now, I don't have to think about it. I get my S.A.V.E.R.S. done before 7:00 a.m., every single day. The book says to master your life, and this and that, all before 8:00 a.m. I was always a night owl and never liked using an alarm clock, let alone waking up early. I still find it funny that I now get up at 4:30 a.m. and complete all my S.A.V.E.R.S. by 7:00 a.m.

By the way, part of the belief and value factor we talked about earlier includes not telling yourself negative things every day nor verbalizing your inhibiting beliefs. That would be "self-talk," which is a crucial part of a Good T.A.L.K. and is so important that it is the title of Chapter 5.

Silence is Golden

S.A.V.E.R.S. begins with the letter S, which stands for "silence." I'm a very spiritual, Godly person. Some people call it religion or being religious. It's ultimately just the unprecedented, 100 percent faith in God and my relationship with Him. It's as real to me as this book. When I wake up in the morning, my silence is just a form of gratitude, giving thanks to God for another day. Then, I chug that glass of water, placed there the night before, because health is important. A lot of people don't know this, but as you've been sleeping, even if you drank water before bed, you wake up dehydrated, which slows you down. I follow that by reciting a long prayer (for me, it is the same one everyday), which takes about ten minutes.

People say, "Well, I need coffee. I need this." Well, that's inhibiting belief number one. You will do, have, and be, whatever you tell yourself. So, if you keep saying that you need coffee to even talk to somebody, then that's going to be the truth. But chemically speaking, if you're dehydrated, you're making it harder to be happy, do your daily disciplines, and create these habits. Do yourself a favor and never skip the water. Chug it right away. That all falls under the S of S.A.V.E.R.S.

Life-Affirming Action

The A is for "affirmations." For me, in my job as a real estate professional, I need to know what my clients need and what is important to them. A little bit of early-morning social media gets this done very effectively while simultaneously, in the background, I'm playing self-recorded affirmations that increase my personal belief in myself and is a constant reminder to my subconscious what my core values are. These recordings feature a mindset and attitude I want to carry with me that day, something really good about myself, or things that I'm grateful for. It's probably a good fifteen to twenty minutes of recordings of my voice affirming what I want to be, do, and have—things that I believe in, love, enjoy, and that are important to me. These are playing in the background while I'm looking at these random feeds, whether it be Instagram, LinkedIn, or Facebook. Meanwhile, I'm listening to my own core values and beliefs, which is sending positivity out to the world I am observing. Those are powerful—just like the other letters of the S.A.V.E.R.S. you're about to learn. You must affirm your daily core beliefs—things that you ultimately believe in, which also add value to your goals—or some other programming is going to activate. We are creatures of habit. Whether they are bad or good habits, we operate off those. So if we're not where we need to be, it's necessary to form better habits to get to the right place!

Getting Your Visions On Board

Now that you've got the S for silence, and the A for affirmations, it's time to learn the V, "visualizations." This is vital—it's your big why. Your visualizations are the physical picture of the things you want to do, be, and have—what you love and is important to you. Maybe it's even similar to a bucket list—things you want to do before you die. Actions or events that bring joy to your life.

Create a vision board. What I did was choose eleven core things that are important to me, and then I pinned them onto the board and hung it in my room. Funnily enough, when I first started, even though these were goals I knew I would love to accomplish, I couldn't remember all of them. So, again, I had to apply the discipline of staring at the board and getting it right. Now, I can spit out the story of all eleven in less than a minute, and I can see the board as if it's right in front of me when it's not. It's those visualizations which remind us what we crave—the wealth of HA.HE.WI.WE.

Notice the connection here. All these chapters are going to link together. Because when you speak in principles—which I love to do in addition to using core values—most of the time they will work the same way right across the board, no matter what you're doing. Now, technically, you don't have to follow along in this order. After you wake up in silence, you may do your visualizations, listen to your affirmations while you exercise, and then read after you've written in your journal. The main thing to do is identify your routine and do them in an order that works for you.

Exercise Your Right to Be Healthy

That brings us to the E in S.A.V.E.R.S., "exercise." That's part of the healthy qualities of HA.HE.WI.WE. You have to do some sort of physical activity or you're literally telling your body that you're giving up. Our bodies are designed to be mobile. However, genetically, we were not prepared to be able to fly our own planes anywhere and whenever we wanted, drive to anywhere, or be able to order a hundred hamburgers and eat them all within ten minutes. We didn't have the time to kill enough cows to do that, tens of thousands of years ago. Our resources have changed a bit, but our bodies must still be physically maintained because we're supposed to be able to hunt for food, build a shelter, and fight to defend our family. If we lack that physical ability, everything else has a domino effect behind it. So exercise is huge.

I once thought, "Oh, all I need to do is get enough sleep and eat clean (or as clean as I could)." I didn't do any cardiovascular, muscle toning, or anything to boost my endurance as an adult. It was terrible. I was in a bad mental state, so it was hard to manage my mood. Because I wasn't exercising, it was hard to do my tasks and push through my disciplines and create those habits. So, by exercising, I physically made my body into a better shell for my mind. Now my attitude is better, my energy is better, and so are my sleeping habits.

I start my day with a two-mile run (while always challenging myself to beat my previous time) and a thirty-minute exercise session in my garage before 7:00 a.m. My exercise regimen from Monday through Friday—and I never skip a day—begins right after I've finished my reading. I've done my affirmations. I already have my workout clothes right by the bed. After slipping my shoes on, I do some stretches to get ready for my run.

Once I'm done running, I rest maybe a minute or two, then go right into my routine, focusing on a different type of workout each day. That, combined with my run, gives me a full body workout in my own garage, in my own home, all before 7:00 a.m. I do that every single morning, Monday through Friday. If you believe it may take a lot of your energy away, I will say it does the opposite. This routine gives me enormous amounts of sustainable energy.

Worthwhile Accomplishments Require Action

Again, you're not going to want to do it, but that doesn't matter. What you really want is your wealth that's important to you. You want to achieve or serve your big why, so you must instill these disciplines to make them easier habits. Granted, it became easier to run my one mile, and at some point, I started running two. Sure, those two miles will be difficult at first, so I'll have to tell myself, "No matter what, I'm still going to do it." But I've never regretted it. I've never finished my workout going, "Man, I wish I would have skipped that." That's something you should really take to heart because that should prove to you that it's worth it. Habits don't really get easier; you get better. Matthew 7:13-14 is a great quote from Jesus that says to me, "God didn't ever say it was going to be easy. He just said it was going to be worth it." Let me tell you, those exercises are not easy, but every, single, time—they are worth it. So there's no argument there.

Why do we always think that something's worth it once we've finished it, even if we didn't think it was worthwhile while we were starting? That's our mind telling us not to do it. In other words, there's another voice at play. The voice that talks inside of you is not the same one that makes the decisions for you. That voice would be the narrator—the real you. But you're fighting against the part of your mind that (for the sake of safety and security) wants to do nothing.

Now, in this world of competition and technology, you can't accomplish anything if you're trying to stay safe in your cave with a stick and a flint. You need to get out and be productive. Thriving is the new serving! You need to be happy and healthy. Getting out there to gain wisdom and achieve your goals will set you up so that you can keep doing it over and over.

Reading the Right Stuff

This brings us to the R in S.A.V.E.R.S., "reading." You have to read. I don't mean Harry Potter or Dr. Seuss. I mean subjects that align with your values, beliefs, goals, and career—the things you want to do. Maybe the things that you're not good at that you want to get better at—like a special trade. Twenty or thirty minutes spent reading a motivating, uplifting, and business-building book gives you some new knowledge to start your day—a new story to think about. Perhaps you're reading a book for the second time. Maybe you already know the value of the book and you've just forgotten it. Reading fills you with the right stuff.

There are times though that you think, "I can live without it." However, very rarely do I read thirty minutes of something and think, "Ugh—that was a waste." There's always one little nugget to latch onto. There have also been moments where I've got tears in my eyes. Other times, I read something so impactful and profound that I actually am in tears. Literally, by myself, in my house, it's seven thirty in the morning, and I'm in tears because of something that resonated with me—and now I can carry that wisdom throughout my day. It's important that you read something—like a ripping-good book, a book very much like this one!

I don't recommend audiobooks. They're great at night or in the car because it takes less energy and it's a more efficient way of absorbing knowledge, but in the morning, tap into your reading skill when your body is at its peak potential. Get those eyes moving and peruse as many pages as you can! Reading is the *wise* of HA.HE.WI.WE., so the more wisdom we can take in, the more fruit we can share, and the greater our wealth becomes.

Scribing Your Goals and Your Life

Rounding out your S.A.V.E.R.S. is the S, "scribing"—writing out and illustrating your day and your goals. Keep a journal. Again, this is not a subtle suggestion. You have to do this, or none of this will work. You keep a journal by your bed to make things easy for yourself. No sense in fighting against yourself. Make sure there are no obstacles in your way—give yourself reasons to do it right, and do it consistently!

But you have to journal things that are amazing in your day. Things that are extraordinary, goals that you want to achieve, something you learned, or an experience you had, and what makes you grateful. You want to affirm them all by recording the story of your life. When you do that, not only is it going to be a fun read fifty years from now, and something to give to your children, but in your mind, you're releasing the old and adding the new. The biggest thing that does is keep you on the right path.

If you can write out those goals, accomplishments, or things that you want to do, you are moving forward and putting the bad behind you. You can build on what you've gained from anything the day before, and then grow and do something more impactful and more influential. So, writing down your goals and your accomplishments each day—almost like a diary—is powerful and absolutely cannot be skipped on a weekly basis.

It's better to journal every day, but there are some days where you can't really connect the story, so I get it. If you would rather do shorter entries every day, great, but at the very least, you must pick the same morning every week to connect your path in the journal consistently. Your daily disciplines we talked about—the good news is they all get done before 8:00 a.m. Don't tell yourself you can't get up early. When it comes to S.A.V.E.R.S., do whatever you are willing to do. You can do the S, the A, the V, plus the E, R, and S—your silence, affirmations, visualizations, exercise, reading and scribing—all before eight in the morning. And you can change your life for good!

SELF-TALK

How you communicate with others starts with how you communicate with yourself. I'm not trying to turn this into a self-help book, but I do know that there are some fundamentals required to build the foundation of good communication. These first five chapters include the disciplines required for that. Last, but not least, is self-talk.

I hear people all the time telling me who they are and what they can and can't do. I'm here to tell you that nobody can possibly know what they're capable of unless they try over and over again. To always walk around declaring what you can't do—or what you can do—sometimes limits you, mentally speaking. It's simply a waste of time. Even if you truly are not, and you don't have any desire to be good at something, by saying that, you're keeping yourself in the same boat. So you must either avoid mentioning anything negative like that at all, or commit to not being that person. Let's say that one of the things you like least about yourself is that you are too hard on yourself. Well, to switch that around, do the opposite of negative self-talk, positive affirmations. Simply say that you are good at those things. You are good at talking to people and saying positive things. You do give yourself every right to make a mistake. It is the same as Henry Ford's classic saying, "Whether you think you can or you think you can't, you're right." Choose wisely.

Correcting Without Condemning

Mastery is to realize you are the clay, not the potter. You must be able to correct yourself without invalidating or condemning yourself. You want to accept the results to move forward and grow toward mastery.

I always say, "Be careful what you say to yourself and how you define yourself." When you argue for your limitations, as Gary Keller would say in his book, *The One Thing*, you keep them (your limitations that is). We call those "inhibiting beliefs." Challenge those negative beliefs and doubt your doubts. Give yourself credit to know you can accomplish anything—get through anything. There is no problem too great to overcome and no win-lose. There is only a win and learn.

Like exponential growth, one could say, "We grow through what we go through." What you struggle through, just like in battle—the mental axe-sharpening, the situational tragedies—makes us better, bigger, and more capable of handling more and greater accomplishments. Not only that, but you can handle and overcome more of the problems better—leading to better results.

I can't stress enough how important it is to realize that negative self-talk can hurt you, and on the other hand, how much positive affirmations can help you. Never define yourself as anything but capable and willing, no matter what it is. Even if you haven't yet tried it for the first time.

Confidence, Competence, and Fears

Let's talk a bit on the subject of fears. What they mean, what the absence of fear is, and a little technical stuff about communication. People are often held back while communicating simply by fear. Maybe you're speaking in self-talk which doesn't truly exist. For example, a lot of people fear public speaking. Do you realize there's really no threat when speaking in public or in front of audiences? You're just not capable of it yet, so you lack confidence. But in truth, if you're reading this book, you may be looking for more competence and confidence in communication.

Most people, no matter what their chosen field is—whether they're doctors, lawyers, real estate agents, sales executives—part of what they do is apply their expertise. The other part is lead generation—finding a client to sell to. If you're a doctor, you may be selling yourself to a medical board of directors for a new job working at a different hospital. You may not be selling yourself to the person who needs a heart transplant, but you're selling yourself to somebody at some point. We're all in the lead generation business. It's not what you know, how much you know, or even how long you've known it—it's often who you know. It's important to see it that way when looking at communication in any field.

Negative self-talk is the biggest inhibitor I see in people when communicating with them. Even someone I'm not training or coaching—someone that's on the other side of the deal with me or even a customer—says things about themselves, or their house, or what they can't do. I'm here to tell you that part of good communication, confidence, and competence is really all about starting from a position of love—loving yourself and being confident in yourself and your capabilities. For me personally, I have a divine connection to my Lord and Savior. A lot of my confidence comes from knowing—like the message in the poem *Footprints in the Sand*—that through the hills and the valleys and the highs and the lows, my mind will be cleared and cleaned by the goals I have set for myself through my faith. That's important to me. That's the source of my confidence. What is yours?

This book isn't about self-help and it's not pointing anyone in any religious direction. However, I will share my faith with you because having core values is the first step toward no longer constantly judging yourself and everyone and everything around you! It's the source of my competence and a lot of the ideas found in this book. So remember, the biggest inhibitor to your progress and communication is your own self-talk. It's whatever you're repeating to yourself—out loud or in your own head over and over again. Be very conscious of what you say, how you say it, and how it makes you feel. Your feelings are the magnifiers of your thoughts, and that's what embeds those codes into our brains to give us our own opinions and judgments of everything in our lives. It all starts with good, *positive* self-talk.

F.E.A.R.
(FALSE EVIDENCE
APPEARING
REAL)

Reprogramming Daily Disciplines

Fear has been talked and written about so much that it is almost cliché, but it is still the number one thing that holds people back from becoming all they want to be and having all they want to have in life. However, since most fear only exists in our minds, we can reprogram our fears with actions. F.E.A.R. and daily disciplines go hand in hand. When someone fears what they're doing, whether it's entering a new career, pursuing a new lead, or anything they're not familiar with, they won't bring that necessary confidence if they're not already practicing daily disciplines. In other words, I don't mean practicing script and role play, but daily disciplines that will make us better at what we're supposed to be doing to give us better results.

Take, for example, real estate agents. Imagine a listing appointment, which includes specific questions that will help you learn important information about the client as well as a clear plan of action that delivers predictable results. Having a set concept to follow will develop the confidence that's going to eliminate the fear of meeting a stranger and then explaining what we're going to do to sell their property. Maybe you've been in medical sales for fifteen years and you have a new challenge. You're selling manufacturing parts to somebody who develops a bigger product, using multiple products and bits of technology. You're going to apply the same principles, but if you don't have the daily discipline to gain the familiarity you need—whether it be for the specific product or your own psyche—you're not going to be at top performance.

Fear, in general, is really nothing at all. It's a lie. It's based on our fight-or-flight response, which originated from growing up in a world where you had to fight for your life. Fear has carried us through thousands of years, but with the wisdom and understanding we've gained, fear (in most cases) can and should be replaced by knowledge, but you have to believe.

Daily Disciplines Will Boost You

What if I told you that even the daily discipline itself is enough to get started? It won't be something that you have to suffer through or deal with for the long term. Most people feel that when they start something, it will always be as difficult as it feels right then and there. Subsequently, they tend to believe that when it's not difficult anymore that it's not as significant. It is worth repeating that the daily disciplines you do, whether they be to help you on a personal or mental level—or to understand your product, client, service, and objective—will boost your confidence until it oozes from you.

It's going to take practice, just like anything. Start with the S.A.V.E.R.S. in the morning, of course. That will help you with the mental side of things. Others would teach script and roleplay to adopt foreign skills. However, you can see that by beginning with the right mindset, you correct the problem at the source *for good*. It will generate results and give you the energy and attitude you need to achieve what you are really after. Having those disciplines are what matters, as well as understanding the short-term power of discipline.

Remember that humans are creatures of habit, so you can't do something like this only once. No single attempt or action could possibly sustain a goal or desired area in life. If you want to work out and build muscle, you can't go to the gym once and stay that way forever. You have to go every day. When you stop, what happens? Your muscles start to get smaller again. We are indeed creatures of habit, whether it be physically, mentally, or spiritually—what we're able to do as far as activities in those categories regularly defines who we are as human beings.

You place a seventy-year-old man on a bicycle, and if it's been a while, he might not be as adept as he was when he was younger because everything requires daily disciplines to maintain and improve. It is so easy for us as average humans in today's society to assume that we know what we need to know to do well and grow. Upon doing it once, we classify it as boredom or too easy, and we never do it again. We miss understanding the fundamentals of a lot of success in the choices that we make and the things we do.

Fear is a huge part of that. Fear, next to love, is one of the strongest emotions we have. What I have learned over the years, in all the books that I've read, is that fear and love are never in the same space. As a verb, if you are truly showing love to another, you are not afraid. If you love something, someone, or some act, then you certainly don't feel frightened. The good news is that love is stronger than fear. You don't even really consider any potential fears because your love of that act, person, or thing is far greater.

Reprogramming Your Beliefs

Reprogramming is all about removing the old and letting in the new. I've known so many people who were so close to greatness, but sadly, they just held onto who they were, and nothing in their life ever changed.

I remember a couple of those people telling me, "You know, I don't want to listen to that, and I don't want to be brainwashed. I'm not going to change my mind or forget my morals or beliefs." That's not what reprogramming is. Not at all. My faith is stronger than anyone I know, and yet I also know the power of reprogramming. Because when you lead with faith, when you lead with biblical principles, you develop values that never change. The core values developed through a faith, whichever you have chosen, will be the anchor for all your decisions. The reprogramming, in a sense, is just altering the decision-maker, the perspective in which you see things. It's a real thing. You can undoubtedly change your own beliefs and your own self-talk, just by affirming those things to yourself daily. Don't be afraid to let go of the old you and bring in the new!

Albert Einstein said that the definition of insanity "is doing what you've always done and expecting different results." If your thoughts and attitude aren't leading you to where you want to go, you're going to have to rethink why you're looking at these scenarios in a certain way, or your life will truly never change, and neither will your communications. You can read this book a hundred times, but until everything in you—your inner and outer self—truly believes it, it's never going to work for you. That's because your conscious self and your subconscious self must be in alignment with the rules, values, actions, tasks, and principles of your goals and visions of your future.

I've learned numerous concepts over the years that I will share with you, but they never yielded any results in the past because I truly didn't believe them. I didn't believe they would add the value to my life that they actually do. Once I started to believe them, once my inner and outer self-aligned, I realized the value in it, and my practice and daily disciplines built my confidence to do them. That's when the results started coming to fruition. I started succeeding at an extremely high level, and with a big smile on my face.

Eliminating F.E.A.R. (False Evidence Appearing Real)

You must be fearless. We don't see the things that truly wreck our lives. We have no idea that they are coming, we know nothing about them, and we're not prepared for them. When it comes, it's almost never a fear that's been on your mind, and it's never something that could happen in a transaction, deal, or sale. The things that scare us the most—mentally beat us up—typically never happen. Eliminating fear is all about truly progressing past the self-talk and appreciating and understanding daily disciplines.

Remember that most human beings will always underestimate what they can do in a day, and overestimate what they can do in ten years. Don't be afraid of what you can actually accomplish in a day. Even if it doesn't lead to instant gratification, those days are connected and they add up. Like your exercise in the morning for S.A.V.E.R.S., it might be beating you up. You're afraid and think, "What if I hurt my leg and I can't walk?" Those fears may become a reality simply because you're thinking about them. But a fear like that would stop you from your daily discipline, leading to more excuses—and more of the same thing.

If you're afraid of something, bring love into the situation—how much do you love it? If you're afraid of making that call, how much do you love what you do and helping other people?

Hard Choices for an Easy Life

Here is something else worth remembering: *Our greatest desires, our greatest glories that we long for, are on the other side of our greatest fears.* So, if you could imagine a decision to be made and a wall in between you and that choice—that's the fear, and the result of your persistent action will reveal the greatest thing you could ever hope for, and that's almost always how it works.

It's like riding a roller coaster. Everyone's freaked out the first time, or if it's been a while. You might tell yourself, "I don't know how I'm going to feel this time." Or maybe, "I'm a little older; my equilibrium's messed up." Or, remember going on that daunting fairground ride when you were a kid. How many people go on a roller coaster, freak out, and vow to never to go on one again? Almost nobody, but you still fear it. You're still scared of the unknown or what you don't remember.

Think about skydiving. Everyone's afraid until they jump. If I asked a hundred people who had just parachuted out of an airplane, most would say, "Oh my goodness, that was the most fun ever. I can't wait to do it again!" However, if you ask anyone who's never done it how excited they are to go, you're going to get an entirely different response if they don't already believe they can do it or want to do it.

So just remember the power of fear, and then engage in the daily self-disciplines that counters it. These disciplines guide you toward communicating in a way that's most effective, to give you the life you want. Because making hard choices gives you an easy life. Deciding to make only easy choices gives you a hard life. Choose wisely.

PRINCIPLES

Principles Never Change, but Everything Else Must

It's time we talked principles and, indeed, values. A principle, by definition—the way I see it anyway—is something constant. An answer, result, or a meaning that, even with multiple different scenarios, will be the same. Value is similar, but it's a personal thing. It's what you choose to believe and hold onto, or the way you interpret that principle for yourself.

In the same way, principles are found in nature and act as universal laws, like gravity. Similarly, when my ancestors were planting their winter wheat in the fall, they had an old Italian proverb: "Sotto la neve pane," which means "beneath the snow will be bread." After planting wheat in the fall, this family mantra showed the faith my ancestors had in God as they endured the harsh winters before the spring harvest.

No matter how good you are at farming, you cannot overcome these principles of nature. No matter what time of the year, you cannot plant a seed today and harvest it tomorrow. Even if you fully understand everything there is to know about clouds, you cannot make it rain. These principles of nature, the universe, and farming are great examples of what a principle is.

Comparably, a "fact" (although the word itself suggests a higher level of certainty than a principle) is actually less "true" than an actual principle. From a biblical perspective, a principle is a fact from God, but a fact, as we know it, originates from man. Once, it was a fact that the world was flat—that there were nine planets in our solar system, and it was once a fact that cigarettes were healthy. Currently, none of those three facts are true, so stick with principles; they never change.

There are principles in business, and of course, people themselves have principles. Let's say you want to do something nice for somebody. Or you're telling yourself, "Oh! I've got five bucks in my pocket. I'll give it to the next person I see." What if the next person you see is mean to you? Out of principle, you're not going to give that person that five bucks because they upset you. However, if giving in the form of a random act of kindness is one of the core values you have adopted, then giving that person the five dollars would happen out of principle. The truth is we all feel that way, but most of us are not going to do something like that for somebody if we've been insulted. That's a common principle.

And it's something important to know when negotiating. If you don't understand the principle of the transaction, you might end up looking like a fool for asking for certain things without realizing how imbalanced that question is. The win-win or the principle of the situation, whatever it may be, has become unbalanced.

It's also important to understand the other side's intangible leverage—what do they have to lose? What extra leverage could we have, or do we have? That's focusing on the principles of the deal.

It Is Not About You

The other part I like about principles are the values. What are your values? What do you consider to be important in your decision-making? For me, my faith is first and foremost. All the glory goes to my Lord and Savior, Jesus Christ. Those core values include being morally, ethically, and legally sound for my clients, and using my heart to make decisions instead of my brain. Putting smiles before money will always allow me to make the right decisions and leave *me* entirely out of it.

Notice these characteristics don't require some unique skill or special talent. It is a matter of deciding. I understand that my core values have a lot to do with me making the right decisions and controlling my attitude. If I'm a bad agent who can't even pay my bills, and I really need this transaction, it's only human nature for me to—even subconsciously—make more aggressive or passive choices without keeping the client in mind for the sake of saving a deal, whether my client has benefitted from it or not. That's a bad place to be and somewhere you don't want to go with your client.

Whether you're in real estate, traditional sales, headhunting, or anything else, you need to completely leave yourself out of the equation. It doesn't matter what you think as far as opinions go. It also helps you keep an even, positive mindset. You're never arguing. You're never truly angry or upset because it's not about you. Typically, you're not going to get upset, because when you are processing this entire deal and transaction, you're aware that it's not about you. It's about the best interests of the client. Whether you agree with the client's wishes—whether you're a fiduciary-type, responsible professional, or you're transactionally-based, you must have that attitude.

Cooperate and Collaborate

Nature has all sorts of principles of cooperation. Part of what I was just touching on in understanding principles is all about dealing in a fair, win-win scenario. A lot of books and people may say, "Fight, fight, fight! Negotiate! Never split the difference! Kill or be killed! Search and destroy!" In many industries, those are good things. Full-time real estate investors make their money when they buy a property not when they sell it, so price is all that matters. In traditional residential real estate, what matters most is what is most important to an individual client. Real estate agents never work with the same house, client, or market in any individual transaction, so there is never a cookie-cutter approach. What that type of client is trying to buy is a beautiful setting for time and space with family and friends. It's not a resale commodity. It's usually not equitably favorable. It's for enjoyment.

You don't have to always dominate in such a way. You want to cooperate and collaborate with the other side—see what they need. Nature works similarly. When you look at a big oak tree, one side isn't twice as tall as the other. Branches don't compete for sunlight, just as leaves don't compete for the angle of the sun. One's not going to say, "I'm a prettier, bigger leaf than you." They work together. They don't have the fear that humans bring to the table. There's no emotional side, so there's no competition. Things just exist in nature, and that is beautiful. We as people can do the same thing. I always marvel when I see a weed growing through a block of cement. Nature can work so efficiently and accomplish the seemingly impossible without competing.

Breaking Through

Let's now look closer at the wondrous ways a plant functions when growing through a crack in the cement. There has to be a way for light, water, seed, and pollination to get into that crack. Next thing you know—through pollination, sun exposure, rain—a divine form of life has begun. The seed becomes stuck in a wet, soggy lump of dirt. It's not sitting there crying and kicking and screaming because it's stuck. It just knows it has a job to do. It has to live. The trigger is the light. There's enough moisture in the soil to support the pollinated seed. It knows its job; it was born knowing it, just like every other source of life. And again, the light is the vital catalyst for its growth. Now, we say, "in principle, follow the light." When you're trying to decide anything, follow the light and you'll find the answer.

So, maybe you're trying to grow as a communicator, move up the corporate ladder, or you feel like you're in a position that you don't want to be in at all, and you have all these big goals. Again, consider the weed and the block. Most people complain about where they are in life and, ultimately, they just sit there. A little germinated seed doesn't know any better. It merely needs to follow the light. So what does it do? It starts to grow. It roots down in the damp, cold soil. It's not concerned about the six inches of cement. It only knows there's light—that's the trigger, the light. It merely needs to collaborate with its environment to grow.

You and I both know that there's no way there's a plant can push or manipulate concrete. It's just not going to happen. Talk about principles—the laws of physics prevent that. But the plant doesn't need to push the concrete. It merely needs to keep growing. So what does it do? As more rain and sunlight comes through that crack, it keeps growing. It doesn't have to push through the concrete. It shifts its angle to overcome the resistance and finds the gap and then does this continuously without any fear or judgment.

Doesn't that sound just like habits done every day? If the plant gave one good push in the beginning and quit after hitting the first block of cement, those leaves would never appear. But it grows a little bit, every single day. In faith, as divinity would have it, the plant keeps growing until either it can't anymore, or it just bursts open with a big bloom. Almost always, that's exactly what happens.

By the time we see it, that's definitely what happens. The plant has broken through. It's used the crack in the cement to keep it stable, and the flower blooms above the concrete, allowing water and sunlight to be absorbed. And there you go! (See figure on next page.) If something in nature can do that so effortlessly, imagine what we as human beings can do in our lives if we eliminate our fears and doubts and simply follow the light.

Flower of Hope

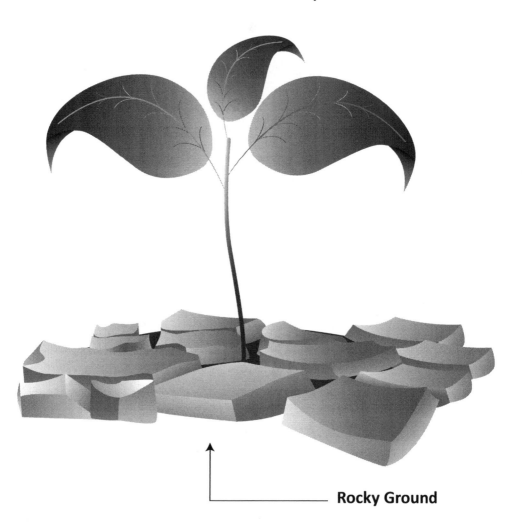

Rocky Ground

GROWTH

Growing Through What You Go Through

When what we go through leads to our growth, we not only have better, more predictable results and maintain a healthier, happier lifestyle, but we can better handle obstacles and stress. This is the growth stage. I'm going to mix a little bit of both nature and divinity into all this. We just finished up principles and values, and now we're onto growth and working again on the mindset.

A little example of handling stress through growth and evolution would be to describe a crying baby. When a baby cries at three months old, it is usually for nothing more than being hungry, tired, having a tummy ache, or a dirty diaper. If we as adults were to feel that way, we may wonder why we have a diaper on, but we would most likely not cry. All kidding aside, we won't cry because we have elevated our mental and physical abilities to a state that can handle that. It just doesn't seem as bad, but if we've got problems with our bills, or our spouses and relationships, our kids, or other major adult issues that we're not prepared for, we will cry the same way a baby does they're hungry, etc. Problems are not really meant to be avoided all day. Instead of avoiding things, what we really need to do is better ourselves and improve our mind. That all starts with confidence and desire!

Letting Go of the Old and Welcoming in the New

Growth is not just about becoming something new and better. It's also about letting go of the old, less capable us. We can't grow and become new, different, and better if we're still stuck on any negative emotions or regrets from the day before. If you want to be better tomorrow, you must say goodbye to the person you were today and yesterday. It is like saying, "If we want to read a better history tomorrow, we must write a better history today."

I know a lot of people don't want to be uncomfortable or have any conflict or discomfort. I once read to that effect, "The biggest threat to progress is not conflict; it's comfort." So our comfort zone—our ease in life—is what resists our growth and any efforts to make ourselves better so that we can do, have, and be more.

Common sense is not always common practice. We not only need to know how to use it, but why, like our big why. We've talked about the *why* and how important it is; you've got to know it. When you believe you can, and you understand the value in doing it, you will do it. You will take the first step.

If You Believe, You Can!

You can read this book a million times. I've reread multiple books and never did anything with them. The moment I found my why—and I hope all of you find it by the time you reach the end of this book—I met a few people who led me to believe that I could do it. And I believed that if I did do it, I would be highly successful, that there was nothing to stop me. You can believe you can do it too, and as they say, when the student is ready, the teacher will appear. You can know it's going to add value, but the more certain you are that it will be done, the more likely you will be to do it.

Certainty is the key to progress. If you knew—simply by reading this book from the first word to the last —that you would have, be, and do anything and everything you ever wanted, would you ever hesitate to read it? No. Not if you got to this sentence in the book and believed it beyond the shadow of a doubt. If you were 110 percent certain that the results you were trying to attain, you could get—you would do it. The missing element is certainty. Because after believing that you can do anything, or at least this one thing, and knowing it's going to add value to your life, all you need to do is be certain that will be the case. Certainty is the catalyst.

Who Remembers Roger Bannister?

As we build people up within, we're going to create leaders. Whether you see yourself as a leader, already are one, or maybe you're part of an infra-structure—know that in leading and understanding growth, you have to look forward. You have to have some sort of vision.

I always like to compare the vision of a leader to a manager. Where I come from, a leader sees clearly. When envisioning a goal, talking about it, or setting up a system to reach a goal, leaders see the target clearly, with pre-set value and certainty. They understand the obstacles and find ways around them and through them. Managers only see the obstacles in the way. They know there's a goal, but all they see are the obstacles, one after another. They manage through that, whether it be for themselves or for others.

There are two mentalities to have in looking at this. There's the leader mentality and the manager mentality. Mentality and your perspective are will define the way you look at everything, so understanding both leaders' and managers' perspectives is vital.

Be Careful of the "My Way or the Highway" Trap

After we have confidence and desire, my favorite philosophy of growth comes down to two things: removing all doubts and starting to answer our own questions. If you want to do anything, perhaps write a book, buy something special, go somewhere, obtain something—the first thing you have to do is remove all your doubts and start finding answers to each of your questions, one at a time. If you do that, you will arrive at your destination 100 percent of the time. Quitting is the only thing that will stop you. Effective communication is the foundation of achieving success in almost any field, which is all part of what we teach in this book. We speak about T.A.L.K. (truth, attention, listening and kindness).

For example, understanding the principles behind these four pillars of communication, and mastering their application, will help you excel in all areas of your life. These philosophies work communicating with others and even oneself. However, so many people self-analyze way too much for too long. If we don't have another human being or two, three, four, ten, or twelve—to bounce ideas off and re-justify, redefine, and reframe every thought that runs through our minds—then we get confused. We tend to unknowingly reprogram our own subconscious brain just by re-justifying and re-understanding our thoughts. So you have to be careful that when you are alone and trying to analyze things, that you run those ideas by a friend, family member, co-worker, or boss. Whether it's about your faith, your job, something great, or something terrible, never let those thoughts be justified and analyzed solely by yourself.

I know it's good to have your own perspective, and a lot of people have the "my way or the highway" mentality—or whatever makes you feel good about being in control. But in the end, it can't be the only thing used to justify, because we can't assume that we know enough never to be wrong, and we must be open to truths. I've known many people that, even in their own faith in God, have become confused and bitter and more depressed just because they've over-penalized and penanced themselves with their faith when it truly wasn't necessary.

So, talk to others. Talk to yourself, but don't do just one or the other. Communicating back and forth is key. That's all part of the Law of Attraction. We'll gain different perspectives and understand some of the faults in our thinking when we share ourselves with others.

Our thoughts and our minds are vitally important, and the thoughts in our heads do not live there rent-free. Whether you know it or not, unless your conscious mind is completely focused on whatever is in front of you, you're always going to have a separate reel of thoughts running through your mind. Those aren't living there rent-free. In fact, they're either one of two things: an investment or an expense. If you're dwelling on the negative, with a pessimist mentality of what could happen, then those thoughts are costing you. They rob you of your peace, sanity, and happiness when they do manifest.

Conversely, when you're dwelling on positive thoughts, thinking about things you love and enjoy, and being optimistic about what is to come—that is truly an investment in your mind and in your future. The first step is to understand and be conscious of your thoughts in that way.

Discomfort = Growth = Success

When you're in growth mode, there's going to be a lot of doubt. When you're in grade school, there's always a little bit of tension because you're constantly in a state of limbo—a state of taking what you know and making something new or learning something you don't already know. So there's an exponential factor in education. Grades, from kindergarten through the end of college, apply that bit of discomfort that cause growth. If we aren't applying pressure that way, when we get out of college, then we become stagnant. We stop that exponential expansion, and it is the kind of discomfort that is part of growth.

Think about trying to grow muscles. Does it happen just by looking at them and smiling? No! It happens by beating them up in the gym and breaking them down. Our personal growth is no different.

There is a great anecdote about growth as it relates to nature. It's important to realize this comparison because it lets us get a better visual of the process and define it. Now, there's a lot of symbolism around the eagle— the way the magnificent bird soars. If you're from America, you're familiar with the way the eagle symbolizes the United States. But then, take life and nature down to its smallest little element, and it's even smaller than an egg, like a seed.

There are five stages of growth in nature that are great analogies for growth as a human being. Stage one would be the seed of life that grows through the rock. We all are born as seedlings. We all begin with very little information in a certain environment that most of us would call that home. That's when we learn things and we grow.

Bamboo and You

I call the next stage the bamboo phase. This is almost like your teenage years—your adolescence and growth. You're looking at the world around you and trying to make sense of it. You can't really accomplish much at this time, but you can create and sustain a foundation for huge stratospheric success in life. That is similar to the bamboo plant.

After planting the seed of the Chinese bamboo, you can water and nurture it, cultivate and fertilize it. You just keep watering it and doing all of these daily things, but what you'll notice is, above the ground, nothing happens. There are no visual signs of growth. There's no sprout. There's no little mini bamboo that has started to grow. What is really happening is that the bamboo itself is growing its perfectly designed roots horizontally below the ground. The base of the root and stem of the bamboo itself actually grows down into the earth away from the sun. Just below the surface, it grows straight down for four to five years.

In watering it—from a biblical standpoint, in nature—it grows in faith. So as the rain is hitting it, there is nothing visually happening. If a farmer, ignorant of these facts, were to be watering his plant, he might think that the bamboo is not even going to grow, but after five years, once the plant has its genetic code implanted, and the right depth to sustain growth, it begins to grow upward. But now it's all based on deeper, wider, sustainable roots, for maximum growth. As human beings, if we choose to skip that process, if we choose to cut our education and relationships short, jumping from career to career, we're not going to create a foundation for growth like the bamboo has.

From Caterpillar to Butterfly

The next is the caterpillar/butterfly stage. This is when life really starts to kick in. This is the metamorphosis from an adolescent child, to an effective, efficient, life-giving human being who is ready to help others—ready to share with others and grow within. So within the vegetation, from the seedling below and the bamboo plant, a nice little caterpillar devours all the leaves it can get, because that's what it does!

But a caterpillar can only exist as it is for so long. So what does it do? It adapts to its environment to get more out of it—and to give more back. Then it sticks to the plant after it's filled its belly and spins itself a little web, and in a short time, it will grow into an entirely different creature. It has changed itself after thinking, "I'm in this environment. I've done all I can do and there's nothing else I can do. Even God, divinity, and nature say I've got to change."

So, we as humans first graduate high school. We go onto graduate college and then get out into the world. Now we've got to learn a specific trade because we have to take this foundation and make something wonderful with it. Just like in the books, nature says you become a butterfly! Then, a short time later, the butterfly hatches and begins to pollinate the flowers that bloom in the area, doing what it's supposed to do. It gets more value for itself and gives more back to its environment. In reading this book and changing the way we think, and growing from the caterpillar mindset to the butterfly, we can begin to see how everything is connected.

Bee-ing Cooperative

The next example would be the honeybee, a truly incredible creature that is born to collaborate, work, and conserve. It's born to be loyal and take care of the queen bee, designed to be part of an entire workforce. It does not gluttonously consume pollen day in and day out until it can't breathe. The nature of a honeycomb and the storage of honey exists because of the Earth's cyclical seasonality. We don't get spring year-round. There are periods of hardship when the flowers are blooming for only three or four months.

Then what do the bees eat? Well, the only way for them to survive is to prepare. They learn to harvest and store what they need to get through the hard times. This spotlights the evolution of life and the divine nature of adaptation. The butterfly has evolved from a caterpillar into a beautiful specimen, physically, but the honeybee shows you the intelligence within nature. The honeybee can work together with the others, feast when it's time to feast, and store when it's time to store, and so they live and in turn give life.

Eagles Rise Above

Last but not least, the fifth stage is the eagle. This magnificent feathered being is the *ultimate* stage in nature. The eagle is beautiful and strong—a hunter and a gatherer. It takes but also gives back. It also soars high above any problems. So in our growth, when we're either heading for a problem or in the middle of one, the eagle symbolizes our ability to gain perspective and rise above.

Know that you can fix and solve any problem that comes your way. The eagle's physical abilities, as well as its instincts, have evolved to help it thrive in its environment. It may take an hour or a minute. It may take a day, month, year, or ten—but no problem is too big. The eagle mentality reminds us of our mission to rise above those problems. Don't let them bring you down. Keep the rain from waterlogging your wings and slowing you. Be confident, be bold, be courageous; in times of pain and trouble, rise above! Soar above the pain and make your life and yourself better.

WISDOM AND UNDERSTANDING

The Big Secret for Connecting with People—
Listen To Their Song But Hear the Music, Not the Lyrics

Wisdom and understanding, in a general sense, are about understanding people. The sheer nature of gaining wisdom comes from the principles of T.A.L.K. in the beginning of the book. Listening and seeking to understand, rather than to be understood. When the two can be achieved in both directions, you have communication nirvana.

Understanding people and situations is the beginning of good communication—almost like feeling sorry for your fellow human being. Or like I always say, "I give people the right to have a bad day." So if somebody responds a little bit more aggressively than expected, they may just be having a bad day. It could because they were in a traffic jam or were cut off. It might be something on a personal level. It might be a co-worker, colleague, boss, or client. It could be anything, and it happens to all of us at one time or another. Understanding through the wisdom of knowledge in that specific instance will give you the open mind to communicate correctly.

We, as people, are all in the same fight. Most of us are all searching for the same things—love, understanding, camaraderie, purpose, a legacy. We want to have good, healthy relationships. We have a desire to grow, be impactful, and add value—all those wonderful things. Everybody craves these things, including the person who cuts you off or gets in your way on the road. How about that colleague who's competing for the same deal? The client who doesn't choose you for your service or product? They're all wanting to love and be loved as well.

So, if you can put yourself in the same shoes as another human, you can understand and add more value to that person. Simply because of the affinity—the energy—that you would share with that person, which says, "I believe what you believe, and you believe what I believe. We're like-minded." That really widens the conduit, so to speak, and greatly increases the effectiveness of your communication.

Language Without Words

It also allows you to speak using a different part of your body. Most people think that when they communicate or make decisions, they're mainly using their brain. In reality, they may use their brain when they're by themselves and making a calculated decision. But when you communicate from one person to another, the major organ that you are using to make decisions—whether it be conscious or subconscious—is your heart. The heart is equipped with far more nerves than even the brain. The physical tissue of the heart contains more neural pathways and has more neurological computing power than our brains. Our hearts communicate both by receiving and giving these neural pathway signals. In fact, the first sign of human life (the first developed organ) in the human body is not the brain, it is our heart.

We, as people, can send and receive these signals. When you are speaking truthfully and compassionately to another human being, even if you're just listening, what connects you both is the heart. So, when trying to understand the subtitle of this chapter, "When you listen to someone's song, hear the music, not the lyrics," I don't mean that quite literally. When you sit down with a client, or you're doing a needs analysis of a concern your wife or child has—or a client—they're going to tell you something. There's a meaning behind that something, a why, an emotional feeling, and it's about not having the ability to connect visual with tone and tempo, and with the words they are saying that causes misunderstanding

But their words may be encoded in many things for many reasons. There may be something they're hiding that they don't want to confess, something they are missing, they don't understand, or thoughts they're not willing to give up. So, the words that you hear are only part of the story. When you connect with somebody on a level like I am speaking of here, you sense that there are other things involved. You listen for other things—changes in tone, goals, feelings, and emotions. You learn to ask the right questions and to dig deeper, and find out why.

Little Signals Are a Big Deal

The little signals revealed to you, like in their words or changes in their tone of voice, provide you with the knowledge to ask the next, correct question. In doing that, you avoid prematurely wrapping your conscious thought around what the problem is or even what the solution is, because you're listening not to what they say, but rather what they mean.

When you hear someone's *why*, it can be like they're singing you a song. Basing the solution on the words they say is hearing the lyrics. Basing the solution on *why* they said something and not *what* they actually said is hearing their music. Whether it be the beat of drum, the strum of a chord, or the tone of a key, that is their *why*, any that is most important.

For example, if somebody says they want a big, fenced-in backyard, you might think it's because they have a dog. However, what they really had in mind was the problems they had with nosy neighbors with ugly houses. So you don't consider anything without a fenced-in backyard, or houses with Home Owners Associations that don't allow dogs. In reality though, if you could solve the heart of this problem, a security or privacy issue, you may find the actual, correct home for them. It wouldn't slip through your fingers because you were searching for only a house with a fully fenced-in backyard.

The problem may come that those clients don't like any of your suggested homes, and there are not many other options. In their frustration, they may start going to open houses to check out the inventory. One day, they walk into the home of their dreams and find the exact type of backyard they're looking for. This would mean that the agent at the open house would get the sale and you would get nothing!

The answer was a different kind of fence. In this case, shrubs, bushes, or hedges gave them what they were looking for. A bad agent would concentrate only on the fence and just assume it's because of a dog, only searching for houses with fully engaged, locked-in fences at any particular height. Knowing your client's *why*, and not their *what*, helps you understand them on a specific basis. I call it listening to their song and hearing the music, not just the lyrics.

"RELATIONSHIPS"

Plant, Nurture, and Cultivate Better Professional and Personal Relationships

When I say "relationships," I mean in a professional sense, but with a personal touch. This is not a sales book nor a lead generation book. This is not information about conversion rates, closing pitches, sales techniques, or closing tactics. This entire book is about how you can use good communication to develop personal and business relationships.

The No-Network Effect

The "no-network effect" is how most small business owners, realtors, and other sales professionals market and perform the duties of their business. For example, let's say that you're not into building relationships or getting referrals. You have a pool-cleaning service, and you are not a people person or would rather not bother with them. You don't even really have a brick-and-mortar store, so maybe you work out of your garage. You're shy and introverted and new to this business. Most people just use their work shifts to perform the service or deliver the product, sell that in the form of a coupon book, or a direct mail piece, and then survive off of any conversion rates. Even worse, they sit online and focus 100 percent of their marketing on posting noise about what they are selling. That style may feed your ego, but it won't feed you, your spouse, or your children very well. That ends up being a yearly pattern of advertising, converting, selling, closing, and repeating. Over time, as we occupy time and space, things slowly change, including the results or even the once successful habits. That is because by repeating the same process without upgrading your knowledge, or your professional relationships, your individual actions become less effective, which has a negative exponential effect on your mind, body, and your business. If you love what you do, and want to do it for a long time, there is an alternative, and it is much more effective.

Networking Without Working

Have you ever gone to a party or large gathering as a real estate agent, surrounded by people you did not know, and although you wanted to meet everyone for the betterment of your business, out of fear, you chose not to? Then you were left with guilt from your inaction and inability to produce fruit from the opportunity? The bad news is if you did talk to everyone about real estate and what you do for a living, congratulations, you are like every other realtor, but I have good news. Like in traditional marketing, the goal is not to brag about what makes you great, but rather show that you understand your client's greatest need and fear. Similarly, seek to understand the details about your prospect's problem. At that point, if you can establish trust as the wise guide that can lead the client to achieve their goal or solve their problem, while simultaneously giving the client clarity on your process from start to finish, you will actually earn the sale. You will also be able to enjoy a party and not feel obligated to pass out business cards and prevent others from enjoying the party.

The Greatest Gift We Have to Offer Is Ourselves

You may have heard the old saying that people don't care how much you know until they know how much you care. If we are to genuinely care, we must always aim to attract clients by showing them how much we care. However, most agents wait until they are desperate for a sale and then they just cold call, door knock, or lie and beg to get a deal or a listing. I don't think you need statistics to see the reality of that statement. The key is never doing anything that violates your values or principles, and if you don't know what yours are, the first step is to find out, write them down, and review them to yourself daily. In reality, being aware of where you are and what you are doing in the present is a great way to stay genuinely happy and compassionate in a way that doesn't even feel like work.

In my opinion, on any given day, we would be exponentially improving our life if we are always doing one of the following four things:

1. doing what we love that bring us joy;
2. doing things that are important with people we like or love;

3. taking care of ourselves by eating healthy foods, exercising, and reading good books daily; and

4. helping our neighbors and clients solve their problems or achieve their goals.

There are only so many hours in a day, and there are many levels in an organization and company that work together to produce results on a massive scale. As a realtor, most of us are a one-person show/organization, but the flow of a larger real estate organization still makes the process more effective and efficient by definition. However, if we don't have those positions filled by other people, we are either doing them inefficiently, or we are not doing them at all. The person most affected by this circumstance is the client (the homeowner). Over time, the less value we give to the client, the less value the industry holds. If we are to prevent an industrialized "do it yourself" real estate industry that would take money away from good people who give good service to their clients to give a better life to their family, we must bring back the value of face to face, arm's length service that creates a better experience and better results for the client.

That being said, networking works two ways. It allows us to build influence with the local buying and selling community to generate more opportunities to serve clients, but it also allows us to join forces with other vendors and professionals that support the real estate industry as well as buyers and sellers. For example, a client will have many needs during the home buying and/or selling experience, many of which do not fall within the guidelines of our own real estate license. However, a client in need is a client indeed, and real estate sales is truly a people service business. It is important for every realtor who wants to do this for the rest of their career to team up with the best local vendors and professionals to offer more options and better service for their clients.

Here is a personal example of the power of networking, and it can be best described by first asking a homeowner why it is usually better to own than rent? All things being equal, ownership is exponentially more beneficial than renting. When finding a service that your client needs in a hurry, rather than playing "Google Roulette" and putting your reputation on the line, build a team of vendors and professionals that you have previous experience working with, ones who have proven their worth and commitment. They're in it for the long haul, motivated by a give and take relationship of referrals. This motivation especially affects the service you give to your clients through those professionals with whom you share referrals.

I had a client that was throwing a big party at her home on Christmas morning. She had planned on getting her bathroom renovated weeks before so it would be ready when company arrived. In the end, she was unable to get anyone to help her. She called me, and I called my handyman in my net-working group. What happened next could never and would never happen by simply looking up a company and calling them for service, and if by chance someone was willing to do what my handyman did, they would charge an arm and a leg and take at least half upfront (right before Christmas). When a relationship is created, the Law of Reciprocity begins to take effect. Professionals will work hard for you either because of business they will get in the future or gratitude for business they have received in the past, and that has value. A lot of value.

So, I called my handyman on December 15th and told him that I had a client who was in a pickle. She needed her entire bathroom remodeled—new tub, shower, ceiling, fixtures, vanity, toilet, mirrors, closet, and all new paint and base. The handyman came over to the client's house the next day. He did a full evaluation and gave an estimate on the work. The price was far below any quote she had received, but that is not even the best part. After creating a list of supplies that both the seller and handyman would share in getting, work began just a few days later. At this point, it was about December 18th and Christmas was one week away. Being that most people (including handymen) enjoy visiting family during the holidays, taking vacations, or even last-minute shopping, we could not get anyone else to help during this time.

A few days into the work, the handyman was not sure he could finish in time even if he worked on Christmas day, so he ended up hiring another helper along with his son and father who were equally skilled in bathroom remodeling. On Christmas Eve, there were three men (and three generations of men) in the client's bathroom installing tile, fixtures, the tub, the shower, the toilet, the vanity, and finishing up with all the trim and paint. In the end, they finished the bathroom that night and went home on Christmas Eve hav-ing worked day and night the week before. They didn't even invoice the client until after the new year! I can honestly say that the results my client received came 100 percent because of the networking I created years before—because of being willing to share myself with others who are trying to do the same as me for their clients and their family. Networking creates a bond between people that says, "I believe what you believe, and I want what you want." We serve our clients, and when we find a need of theirs, we connect them to an expert we know in that field, and by the time the client meets them, the only question is usually, "When can you start?"

By making those connections, we foster beautiful relationships. So, for all of you who have a database, large or small, and don't know who you're going to call when you need a task done, just remember that an established network will allow you to have it done very little money and effort. But it's intentional, focused effort. That's the seed-planting part—the first step in relationships.

Nurturing Relationships

Now to cultivate any relationship, there needs to be continuous and valuable communication. You must learn the needs, wants, and likes of that client, including facts like their favorite sporting event, restaurant, or concert attraction. Maybe their wedding anniversary or their children's birthdays, or their biggest fear from a past transaction or deal. By talking to them regularly about anything they value, you'll be nurturing the relationship.

Social media is a great way to not only show who you are, what you are, what you do, and how you do it, but also absorb information about what's most important to a client. What do we put on these sites? What is most important to us—good or bad? What we don't like most about things, and for a lot of us, what we do like most about ourselves and our life? If we post it, it's important to us. So being vigilant of that—of your clients—is going to help you build relationships. Observing what your prospects or your clients like shows that you care. A lot of times, they will have what your client or prospect needs has nothing to do with the field that you're in. So, you'll help somebody with something that has nothing to do with your industry. (Giving referrals to your professional group) I call it "the networking effect"!

The opposite of the networking effect would be what I was talking about at the beginning of this chapter, with the gentleman who has the pool company—he simply pays for an advertisement and knows what to expect, then repeats the process over and over. That's what I like to call "renting your clients," rather than owning them. Homeowners know the difference in value between renting and owning. If somebody spends money and time on bringing in clients for one-off jobs and repeats the process over and over, they're leasing those clients temporarily. When you build relationships, you're owning those clients, those relationships, and those future businesses.

When you get a client, you make sure to put their interest first, and now you're helping other people with what they need and what's important to them. The human response is, "Well, I gotta pay this person back." If they pay you back in money, it's called commerce. If they pay you back in similar rewards, it's called a relationship, or in this case, a referral.

Learning What the Client Likes

When nurturing and cultivating professional relationships, I am simultaneously learning about people's important events and preferences, like their children's favorite things, their birthdays, anniversaries, favorite sporting events, concerts—stuff like that. Then that gives me an opportunity to share similar information with my clients. Maybe there's a deal on a ticket for a concert that's coming up. As you build a relationship, that might be worth it. Maybe you see a small, cheap gift that resembles something they like that you could give them, like a card on their birthday–not a company branded and typed card, a real, unbranded, and hand-written card like it was going to grandma.

You start with their service, in which case you'll learn about their business and what they do, and you'll give them a referral before you ever get one from them. Giving referrals is also the best way to get them, even if it has nothing to do with the field that you're in.

Maybe, years down the road, you follow-up with former clients to see how they're doing with your product or your service, and by doing that, you will serve them in a way that holds integrity. When you build relationships, you're maintaining your reputation. So everything you do will be at a high level. It's going above and beyond to maintain that relationship, not just succeed in a transaction. That means that you're going to give them your best.

It's like when you go to a restaurant. Tipping exists to reward the quality of service. Without it, restaurants wouldn't be able to survive nearly as well.

Tips keep the quality of the service staff high because those with poor tips would leave. Otherwise, when the boss is away, the cats will play, and we may be living in a world of buffets.

Even the checkout stands in stores—you want to talk about communication? The checkouts at many large stores are becoming automated because people are more expensive than machines. So, if we don't want our entire world to be like the beginning of *The Matrix*, then I think it's important that we start to accept the value of each person.

The Network Effect

But as I'm building these relationships and cultivating them through those other actions—like birthday gifts, giving referrals—I'm setting the stage to not only get referrals from people they know but, when the time is right to do business with them. Then you repeat the process. Only starting with seven people and having those seven people refer you to three others. And those three people refer you to three more. You never spent a penny in advertisement besides what you did to maintain the first seven members.

Regarding real estate, this could have been an open house. It's all about intentional, focused touches to other human beings who care if people care about them. It's not all about an advertisement or exposure. It's about doing something for someone else. If you want to increase your influence and enhance the odds of your phone ringing, take care of other people first, and they'll take care of you with "the network effect." It has exponentially greater effects on your business than any traditional business or advertising model could ever have.

When I say relationships—cultivate, plant, nurture—that's exactly what I mean. Get in front of people and increase those relationships. Add value to them with the emotional bank account "EBA." Cultivate them by giving back first, and then find what you need based on those long-term, strong relationships. Go deep, not wide, into your sphere of influence. Don't simply advertise to hundreds of people and forget about the ones that came before. Now, all you have to do is send thank you cards and postcards to your original seven clients and all the people they referred. It won't be thousands of pieces of mail either. This method is much cheaper to do and maintain.

It's easy to control, understand, execute, and do, and it will impress these clients who assume you're doing this with hundreds of people. But by focusing on depth over width, you've maximized your dollar per hour. You've made yourself feel better along the way. You've been more effective in what you're doing, and the leads are so much better and at a higher quality in a less stressful environment. That is exactly what happens when you talk about things that are important to people who care.

11

ADDING VALUE

Harnessing the Law of Influence by Putting the Needs of Others First

Making Deposits in an Emotional Bank Account

Let me explain the concept of an emotional bank account. Any time you have made a connection or initiated a relationship, a metaphorical account is created in which value can be given and taken away. Based on the next interaction, that value will increase or decrease. Let's say that the next time you meet with that person—maybe you were supposed to call them the next day at noon, but you didn't call for two days, and then not until two o'clock. Imagine their feelings as a bank account. Your initial interaction deposited, let's say, a thousand dollars. Well, since your next interaction with that person was after you violated the promises you made, there would be a withdrawal from the emotional bank account (and that had an emotional value of $500). Now that person thinks less of you (and there is only $500 left in that person's emotional bank account). You must now do something better to add back what was lost—what was withdrawn.

The key is to realize that when you build a relationship, you're not always going to be positioned for a home run. So, for every interaction—or what I call the moment of truth—the goal is to make deposits every chance you get with that person. Because the moment will come when they will consider referring someone to you. If they're ready to do a transaction with you, the higher the value that's in the emotional bank account, the more likely you are to get the call.

Your chances will increase if you've regularly reached out to them and said, "Hello." If you've stayed in contact and helped them with their little things, when the opportunity comes to either gain a referral or a deal, you would have built up so much value with that person that you would be the first person they call. Likewise, in a transaction or a deal, you have to be constantly adding value because you will eventually make a mistake. So, if your initial contact with a client or lead brought them value, you've undoubtedly made the listing itself more appealing, or maybe you've already gotten a contract. Then go the extra mile to add even more.

The Gift of Adding Value

The other day, for example, a client was moving some stuff around the house, getting it ready to be listed. A few days later, she mentioned that her back was hurting from all the work she was doing around the house. I purchased a fifty-dollar, heated back massager on Amazon and sent it to her for no other reason but to add value—all to help her back feel better, all while increasing her emotional bank account "EBA."

I know that every transaction is a long road and anything can happen. If you see any chance to add value, do it. Give first. Don't just get by with each relationship and then try to put out fires when something bad happens. Truly listen to your clients, and you will find a solution to their problem. If you don't listen, you're never going to find those opportunities to add that value. So, building that EBA does multiple things. It will not only help the process but also that client's evaluation of you during the contract period and after. If you are prospecting, by building up the EBA, you're almost guaranteeing to get the call when the time is right for that client. Wisdom and understanding are *powerful* when executing all this in the form of communication and building up your EBA.

Communication (by the way) isn't always verbal or visual—it's sensory. There are three types of thinking in the world: auditory, visual, and kinetic. When you communicate—no matter how you do it—it could be through smoke signals, cave drawings, a letter, a phone call, or face-to-face, you have to use those moments to increase that EBA. You have to allow yourself to strengthen the relationship at any cost without it being tit for tat. By truly coming to a situation or starting a relationship with wisdom and understanding (first to give, then to gain), things can become that much easier. So remember, when you hear your client sing you a song, use your heart and listen to the music, not the lyrics. It is the basics behind kinetic thinking and communication. This has a lot of impact on an EBA. because it gives you a direction and a reason. In marriage, a lot of people are only nice to their other half if their other half is nice to them first. There are also people who feel like their mood is dictated by what others do for them. Happiness is a choice, and so is giving to others in a professional setting. So, when we communicate with our clients, the purpose is always to find out what they need and want. Use compassion to connect with them on a deeper level that sights and sounds alone cannot do.

To achieve this goal, you must ask questions. Any time you start a conversation, try using what I call the F.R.O.G. formula—family, recreation, occupation, and goals. I know it seems weird that there's an acronym for just having a conversation, but you want to do it right.

There's a right and a wrong way to do everything. If someone's striking up a conversation with me at my kid's soccer game, I want to make sure I touch on what I know is important to them. Who doesn't want to talk about these things? Who doesn't think the four most important things in their entire life have to do with their family, what they do for fun, what they do for a living, and what their goals are? I don't know of anything more important to a person. So when you communicate, that's exactly what you should talk about.

A Good F.R.O.G. to Have in Your Throat

If you've ever talked to someone who seems awkward, or the small talk comes and goes pretty fast—or there's an awkward goodbye or pause—maybe they can't even think of what to say about themselves, and they certainly don't know what to ask. If they can't remember what they know about you, then where do they go with it? Use the F.R.O.G. formula. If somebody comes up to you at your daughter's dance recital, after their initial greeting, you say:

> "Oh, yeah? That's great! How about you? How is everybody? How's your husband? How's your wife? How are your kids? How's the neighborhood? The house? How are they all doing? What do you do for fun these days? I haven't seen you at bingo or any pictures of you on your boat on Facebook lately. What are you guys doing for fun these days?"

But don't forget to stop and listen; the space between each of those questions could be five minutes. Our job is to stop talking and listen. You've asked about the family and the fun. Next, try:

> "How's work? How's your job? How's that going? Life good? Did you get that promotion, or the new job? Still working at that same place? What's new? Are they hiring?"

If thinking of these types of questions is a bit tough for you, then I suggest sitting down for about half an hour and thinking of some questions for some typical industries. A lot of them are vague enough and would work over many different ones. Try questions about their job and then their goals. You know what's going on in your life. Maybe you're thinking about having kids, or trying to get another job. You can use your own goals in relation to what you've already heard when responding. It also shows that you were listening.

When you listen, make sure they know it. For example, when I show up for an appointment, I'm on time. Because I know how important it is to be punctual, I mention this fact. You can knock on the door, and when they answer, you can say:

"Good afternoon! We had an appointment at three. It's two fifty-five, and I'm glad to be here. Is it okay if we start early?"

As I'm personally a fan of getting the answer, "no," first, you can even say:

"Is it bad that I came early? Is this a bad time?"

You want them to say, "no," and for them to be in control, leaving you just standing there with an awkward look on your face until they ask you to come in. It's a great way to earn a little compassion right from the beginning. By doing this, you're adding value. It's all about the details.

So here we are, trying to realize our goals by using F.R.O.G. Within the span of a short conversation, you've already talked about their dreams and goals. Now you have a ton of information and can use F.R.O.G. to wrap up the conversation. The worst thing you can do is take up too much of their time. We're not even going to get into body language in this chapter and knowing when not to overdo it. Just stop at the "G" in F.R.O.G. and say, "Have a great day! Wish you the best! It was great catching up!" Something like that is great.

What I would recommend is getting to a spot before you forget, and either write it down or make a voice memo, like I do on my phone. Once I get away from that person, I'll speak for one-minute about everything new for them. Now, not only do you have a prospect, but you have valuable information. You know what's going on in their life and what's most important to them. In our business, we then start what's called an eight-by-eight. (Later in the book we will talk about how to apply the eight-by-eight.) You don't have to wait until you have a deal or get the referral. The very next day, write them a thank-you card, saying:

> "It was great meeting you. Thanks for the chat." Maybe rerun a little bit about what you talked about. "Hey, I hope this works out."

Building Credits in Relationship Bank Accounts

Done, for now. But don't stop there. Consider doing something for them the next week. You may have heard him say something like, "My wife is going back to school for cooking lessons. She wants to be a chef." Well, how about sending him a reasonably priced cookbook. She might already have it and know every recipe in it by heart, but you listened, and you care, and that's amazing. The book helps build the EBA. Right off the bat, that authentic conversation had a huge impression, but now you've added value to the relationship. Do something a week later, and the next time you see him, just be nice without mentioning what you've done. That's truly because you want to help. That's adding value.

Let's say a month goes by. You've been doing all these nice things for this person, and he's not even close to selling his house. None of that came up in the conversations, but as the Law of Attraction works, you'll notice that everyone has the same type of sphere as you, just different people. Now you've become a major influence in this person's life. Not only do they already now know that they can trust you, but you're involved in what they're doing every day.

That being said, based on the Law of Attraction, somebody is going to come up to them and say, "Hey! I'm looking to sell my house. Do you happen to know a realtor?" Had you not done any of what we mentioned earlier, they would have either said no, or given someone else's name. Now, you've built up that EBA so high that the first thing they're going to say is how great of a person you are. They may even say that though they haven't sold their house yet, but you do great work. They've seen a lot of your other deals. They've known you for only a little while now, and this is what you've done for them already. They might then say:

> "You *have* to call my friend, Robert Paolini. He's wonderful. He can help you with anything. He's very resourceful—he sells at top dollar, and quick, making the process smooth and hassle-free."

I have often said that if no one is thinking about us, we are not doing much, and if they are not talking about us, we are not doing a good enough job.

You've added value to your relationship with that person through what you've done for them. They're enthusiastic, and this sells the referral to the friend. So all you have to do is . . . show up!

Doing good for another person creates relationships with people who, in a sense, become like a warrior, or a bird-dog, advocate, town crier, raving fan—whatever you want to call it. They are the best clients, future clients, and referral-giving part of your sphere. So, whether they need you now or not, or it's a neighbor, friend, family member, or just a casual acquaintance—when the opportunity arises (the moment of truth), will it be you or someone else? When they have to make a decision, they'll consider the time, influence, and help you've given to them, and that's going to reward you tenfold. You're going to get that referral.

Keep Adding Value

There's no such thing as wasting time with another person. You can waste time with things or with yourself, but never if you're adding value to another person. If you're speaking their language in a way that's meaningful to them and doing things that are important for them, then they will always be walking ambassadors for you, your business, and your family. That is what you can build by adding value.

This same concept works in contracts and deals. Always look for ways to add value. If they say, "I want you to do this," do "this" plus one. Do whatever they want plus a little bit more. The plus one was something I took from the book *Raving Fans* by Kenneth H. Blanchard. That's one of the laws; you deliver plus one. Don't over-speak what you're going to do. Don't overpromise and underdeliver, or overpromise and just deliver. Promise what you know you can do, overdeliver, and repeat. That's the way you exceed their expectations, by always doing a little bit more.

By servicing your product and helping your prospects and clients, your value is getting a little bit better every single time. The next time you think about clients, service, and what the heck you're going to do next—if you forget everything else —just remember to add value any way you can. Fill the emotional bank early and often.

12

WORK/LIFE BALANCE

Getting Things Done in Your Life and at Work While Keeping Them Separate in Your Mind

There's a saying that goes, "If you love what you do, you won't work a day in your life." I absolutely love what I do, but that does not mean I can, or should, bring my family with me to work every day. If your spouse is like mine, that is easier said than done, because we have a strong desire to be with our loved ones and that feeling is mutual. That paradoxical effect is why many people have problems balancing life and work. Some say to combine them—others say balance your time accordingly. I once had problems balancing the two, but now I am cured. The problem was that whenever I was at work, I felt guilty that I wasn't at home with my wife and children. Contrarily, almost every day, including the weekend, I would go home and feel guilty that I was not focusing on my clients, staring at my phone, answering texts, or anything to do with them. And if I took a break in the middle of a day or had to go to an event, maybe a sporting or school event for the kids, I would always feel guilty. You won't be happy anywhere at any time if you are stuck in that rut of guilt.

A lot of people try to solve the work/life balance using time. They will say, "I'm going to commit to working nine to five during the week, and the rest of the time, I'm going to be with my family." Some of you might have already tried this and know—it doesn't work. You can't balance work and life using time (at least not in a result-based and 100% commission paid income).

I read a book called *Decide* by Steve McClatchy. It beautifully explains how to truly master a work/life balance and bring peace to your mind every moment of the day. The goal is to be effective and present wherever you are, and you will gain much.

Before we get into the specifics, allow me to share some memories. Some of you might realize how your memory works, and some may not, but I bet you've observed that there are periods of your life that you can remember clearly. Details from whatever happened a week ago elude you, but for whatever reason, you remember things from long ago.

For me, it happened to be when I was in grades seven to nine. At the time, I lived in Central Florida, and that's the only time I lived there before moving to where I currently am. Some of my fondest memories came from those three or four years—wholesome, deep, and detailed ones—that stay locked deep in our reticular activating system (RAS).

Basically, memories only form when we're conscious of where we are. So, we could be out with the kids, or in line at the grocery store, and if we're not actually thinking about what we're looking at or what we're doing, then the memories won't form. There's something running in the back of our heads that is talking to us. It's telling us something, giving us something to think about.

But when you're younger, at that adolescent age, your focus on the world around you is heightened because of hormones. That's when you go from learning everything you need to understanding the world around you, to having the intelligence to consciously absorb information around you to gain more knowledge and make better decisions. The constant search for input to analyze and the desire to gain perspective on the world around us is automatic. That awareness and adaptation is a major part of our survival to this point and our ability to thrive as human beings.

As an adolescent, I was really absorbing the "now," as we called it—the present—wherever you are. I also didn't have the typical stresses that an adult would have, or even a child. When you're young, you stress about little things. When you're older, you have different, more adult stresses—things like bills, health, your children, career, and relationships. Those things detour your thoughts.

It's not usual to find yourself doing nothing, sitting in a dark room, giving yourself plenty of time to think. Yet, there are thousands and thousands of thoughts running through our minds every day. Of course, most of us don't stop. So, if you want to get your memory back, if you want in ten years to remember details like you did twenty years ago, it starts with work/life balance. That means being present—in the now.

The Balancing Act

Now, back to your work/life balance. When you get to work, you commit to a goal. You have a timeframe that designates when you must show up to work. You arrive at your workplace and stay for that duration, every single day. This timeframe includes a period for free time, personal time, catch-up time, etc. But it's all predesigned. Outside of that, you execute your work to the fullest.

Everybody has a long to-do list. You can only complete one thing at a time, so the main thing to do when beginning your to-do list—which should be done the night before—is to prioritize your tasks. In other words, you're really trying to turn your to-do list into "not-to-do" list. You're trying to prioritize the most important first and then rank everything else in the order of most important to least. And the goal is to either delegate or eliminate things that will not be necessary because as you accomplish other important things first, it may render less important tasks unnecessary.

The Bubble Ensures You do the Most Important Task First

This is called the Hoshin Exercise. It's something I learned from one of my business coaches. There's not much about it online. Basically, all you do is take two tasks and draw a circle between them—and that circle is you. The tasks around the center represent your day, and the amount of things you have to do. Then you branch out from the center of the circle to create a bubble chart. You compare two bubbles at a time, asking yourself, "If I could only do this one or this one, which one is more important? Which one should I do?" Then make an arrow from the least important task bubble to the most important. You are comparing only two at a time no matter how many first items are on your list. You count how many tallies are in each circle and put a number by it. Those numbers represent the new priority to focus on for maximum production and effectiveness. This is important because what matters most should never come before things that matter less or least.

See example:

Hoshin Prioritizing Exercise

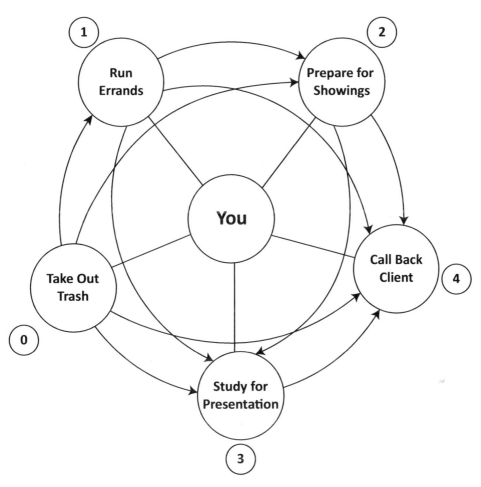

To-Do List

1. Take Out Trash
2. Prepare for Showings
3. Run Errands
4. Call Client Back
5. Study for Presentation

Priorites

1. Call Client Back
2. Study for Presentation
3. Prepare for Showing
4. Run Errands
5. Take Out Trash

Go through all the tasks comparing two at a time until all task bubbles have been compared to all others. You need to be 100 percent honest and consistent with your choices for it to work. In the end, all tasks will each have a different number. Now you just rewrite down your daily goals (tasks) again in the order of the largest number down to the smallest, or what is the most important to the least, and you'll work your way down from there throughout your day starting with the most important task (the most difficult one). Be focused and use your timeline. Eliminate distractions. Have a plan of action. Coordinate your lunch break. Be very intentional with your time.

It might seem like a little bit too much effort. That's just at the beginning, because you're not used to having good habits. You're used to having bad habits. For good habits, you'll need to acquire some discipline, and to do that, you'll have to work on the mindset, which we've talked about. Take care of your mind and your body. Get plenty of sleep and eat well. That alone will boost your productivity for the day. It's also going to allow you to be more effective.

Tell Them When You Will Be There

The second thing I recommend that you do is to record a voicemail message on your business phone announcing what time of day or day of the week you will stop working, and when you will be next returning to business. That way, whoever calls will understand and respect ahead of time what you're doing and why. You won't lose any business because all those days that you were working you did so effectively—because you prioritized everything. You are also more efficient, which creates the feeling of empathy, respect, and understanding toward you with your client. You'll know, even when you're lying in bed alone at night, that you've done the most important things first. And all that you've left behind were the small, mundane things that did not have as much meaning and could be done tomorrow, delegated, or maybe even removed altogether.

That is efficiency at work, and the first step toward balancing work and life. So, when you produce results like that, and you have consistent daily actions regarding your job—be it real estate, finance, a sales job, or anything else—and you've made that voicemail recording to signal when you (as a red-blooded human being) will go home, you do so! This time, when you show up on your doorstep, you've got a big smile on your face. You're happy to see your kids because you know you can leave your work at the office. With your phone in your room, you can really lay back, spread out, and own your time with your family. And if you don't have a wife or a husband or children, it's your time to yourself or with friends. Maybe you like to go fishing, hiking, walking, running—anything. Just do it.

In *The 7 Habits of Highly Effective People*, Covey talks about habit seven— sharpening the saw. If you don't take care of yourself, you can't take care of anybody else. Even on the airplanes, they tell you to put the oxygen mask on you before anyone else. But to sustain a positive mental attitude and a thriving, exponentially growing business, you have to have "you time"—personal time with your family. You have to remind yourself every single day why you do what you do.

Knowing that you're productive at work makes your work-life wonderful, but then that is how you balance both work and your life. When you get home at whatever time you choose, then it's all for your family. You don't think about work when you're with your family, and when you're at work, you don't think about your family because you know that when you're done, you're going to be able to give them 100 percent of yourself. This is where peace comes in for work/life balance.

Juggling Work, Family, and Friends

This is an important subject to understand, as you have certain responsibilities in both work and your personal life, which also includes your friends and your hobbies. Let's pretend that all those categories are balls—balls that you're juggling in the air every single day. You're juggling the balance between your friends who want to hang out, your family who wants to hang out, time for you, your kids, plus private time for your spouse.

Oftentimes, we find that time with the kids and spouse together is not the same as time with them separately. Time shared with each of them is equally important. Personally, the way I look at those balls is that they are all made of rubber except the family one. That one is made of glass. There will always be another deal. There will also be another client. There's always another day to help somebody. Nothing is so urgent in business that it requires immediate attention, for the most part.

Friends—they come and go. Friends sometimes have their own intentions. They start off as acquaintances, but there is an energy or affinity that makes the relationship more long-term—they're going to like you no matter what—unconditionally, but the ball is still made of rubber. There's still a mutual relationship there that is malleable and pliable and can be repaired. But over time, if you are not being present in your relationship with your family—if you drop that ball, there's a very good chance it will break and can never be repaired—ever. You have bankrupted your EBA. Nobody, and I mean nobody, while they're lying on their deathbed many years from now, will regret not working enough nor spending too much time with family. Trust me when I tell you. I've heard enough stories to know that it's the complete opposite. They will always—no matter how much money they earned or didn't earn—want more time with loved ones in the end. In our final hour, it's going to be the time loved ones mean the most to us. Why burn through our entire life? We get one shot at this. We can be exponentially effective in business and accomplish things that most people can only dream while also sustaining a wonderful life with beautiful relationships—personal and professional.

13

SCRIPTS AND THE ART OF BEING YOURSELF

The Best We Have to Offer Another is Ourselves

An amazing book by Bob Burg called *The Go-Giver* teaches the Law of Authenticity, which states, "The best we have to offer another is ourselves." When getting started, what most real estate brokerages teach you are scripts. They use them as the main part of the sales process and most won't have the next step for you to transition to. From the very beginning, they want you to use somebody else's mistakes over and over as your own.

Don't get me wrong. If you are just getting into your industry, you want to have a basic framework for how to communicate in that field. There is also a little rule in real estate: don't practice on your clients. That being said, scripts are great in this way, but that is where their value ends. The principles behind the scripts must be internalized and understood in your own mind—which one, when, where, why, how, and with whom they would and should be used.

Now, yes, success leaves clues. Yes, there's a recipe for success and yes, you save time by following those who have done it before. However, who's to say you're anything like that person and can deliver that exact thing just as effectively? Who's to say, as time goes on, or based on where you live, where you do business, or who your clients are, that it would even work?

My goal is to teach people how to be *themselves* and succeed. You could be an introvert who has never sold a thing in your life and be highly successful in real estate by following these principles. So, throw out the scripts and just be yourself.

A lot of that has to do with what you are willing to do and what you can handle. There are many folks who are great people, but when the rubber meets the road and a decision has to be made, they fall apart. That's another reason mindset is good. Anybody can do anything they want if they feel like it, are inspired, or motivated. It's doing what you should do every day with discipline—things that you maybe don't want to—but you do them because it's the right thing to do that makes you succeed in life.

Taking the Pain Before or After

A lot of people fear pain, and I can understand why. We have always heard of pain and suffering together and most would agree that they are one in the same thing. Somehow, we believe that pain is the source or cause of suffering, so we avoid pain at all costs, but pain leads to growth, so without it, we wander through life with no drive, no purpose, and no success . . . we suffer. The fear of pain keeps us stationary and our lack of action makes us suffer (which our brains confuse as pain). Conversely, if we decide to take action, and welcome the pain, we will then have the internal growth required to succeed. Remember, pain is the first step to success while comfort is the first step to suffering. Like I said at the beginning of the book: pain is required; suffering is optional.

I'm here to tell you that no matter if you are an absolute success in life or a failure, you have pain. The only difference between a winner and loser is the choices they make in life, and the result of those choices. Now, I'm not using the word loser derogatively; I've been in that boat myself! Words don't define us; they describe us! In this case, a person who would consider themselves a loser or a failure is happy with the choices they make, and the suffering that comes from the result of those choices. So, they make easy decisions and have a painful life. But the successful person endures pain every day because they put themselves through it to make difficult decisions. This way they can have an easy, fun, rewarding life filled with choices. You can choose to endure the pain before you do the work or suffer every day you come home from your job.

Even though pain is the common denominator, you get to decide when you want to feel it. Do you want to feel it right away on your own terms? Or do you want to feel it against your terms, when you have no choices, and your back is against the wall?

You'll see the moment you start your morning ritual that it is not fun to get up every day at 4:30 a.m. and do all that work, exercising, and reading, but it's less fun to not have any time, money, or a life of mediocrity. That's painful.

The other day, my child was asking me to play a video game, and he made a funny little remark: "Oh, I wish I could play this game all day." Basically, he was judging, in his mind, that because there's some joy in a video game, technically, if you played it around the clock, the happiness would never go away. Of course, we know that it would. Because if you remember from Chapter 1, society and life (even in nature) do not survive just by *taking*. If you want to play a video game every minute of every day for the rest of your life, be prepared to be by your lonesome for the rest of your days. Now, that's not any sort of life of value, legacy, or fulfillment. It's the easy road. We must perform the hard work to grow and multiply our effectiveness first, and then we can do the fun stuff we like to do. You have to give to receive.

Comfort is the Enemy of Progress

Again, by making easy choices, you have a hard life. If you make hard choices, you have an easy life. Either way, the pain is unavoidable. It's all part of your discomfort while growing. Let's take a lobster for example. Have you ever wondered how a lobster grows? It has a rock-hard shell, but from a small baby to a full-grown adult, the lobster is growing. When it feels discomfort, pain, and pressure, it knows that it's time to molt. The body has pushed so hard against the shell that it can no longer take it. It can't bear the pain. So the catalyst for growth is pain. The lobster hides under a rock and wiggles free from that exoskeleton. Then it grows a bigger one. The point of the story is that the trigger for growth is pain and discomfort.

Comfort is the enemy of progress, not conflict. If you are in a state of discomfort, you're growing. That's why (in this business) we say, "You don't win or lose. You win or learn." Because you're either doing something to progress your goals, life, and business, or you're learning something from a setback or mistake that will cause you to be bigger and better tomorrow. Ultimately, this will continue to give you better growth and better results.

These principles of communication can lead to success in real estate or any other field with communication and lead generation. The book *Ninja Selling* by Larry Kendall (which is part of the "Ninja Nine") shares these principles. The Ninja Nine are specific actions that real estate professionals use that I teach to other agents. However, the best way to describe the difference between the teachings of most real estate agencies and what the Ninja Nine teaches you would be a story about catching a cat. So many traditional techniques revolve around "smiling and dialing." You're calling people again and again at five o'clock or nine o'clock (two of the worst times of the day, in my opinion). Ninety-seven people leave these calls upset. Only three give you a shot, and only one of those might actually lead to a listing or a referral. I may not be a betting man, but those don't sound like good odds to me.

Catching Cats

Now, let's say, for example, that we're sitting in a room together—I, a ninja agent, and you, a regular agent. Somebody offers us a million dollars to catch this cat that's running around the room. It's a pretty big room with chairs, tables, and decorations everywhere. There are a million places for this cat to hide.

What does the ninja do? They concede to the adversary and allow that person to go first. So, you stand up and look at the cat. You hear from the person that's offering the million dollars that you have about fifteen minutes. Immediately, paranoid about the time—and again, not understanding work/life balance and the restrictions that time gives you—you are against the clock. You are already tense and nervous! The pressure is on!

Immediately your nerves kick in; you're hot and sweaty. You start walking toward the cat. The goal is to catch it, but every time you get closer, the cat slowly moves farther away. So you start inching closer and closer. The closer you get, the farther away it moves, and the faster you move, the faster it moves.

Really, you're getting ready to pounce the cat. You're approaching it in a way that is not familiar to the animal—in a way that really has nothing to do with the cat. At this point, all you're doing is trying to get that million dollars, and none of that adds any value to the cat.

You realize the cat is finding little places to hide. Trying to be slow, precise, and clever with your stealthy approach to the animal is not working. So, in anger and frustration, you lunge at the cat, and miss. It quickly darts away. You're throwing stuff in front of the feline, trying to get it to go in different directions and corner it. You're doing everything you can to basically catch this cat without hurting it.

Meanwhile, how do you think you feel? Are you calm, cool, and collected? Are you happy? How do you think the cat feels? Is it excited? Or is it scared out of its mind? Well, you're right. You're miserable, and the cat is scared out of its mind. There's no way you're going to catch it. You're frustrated, you're about to give up, and time runs out.

Now, it's my turn. Here's what a ninja does, and if you can fully grasp this, the rest of the book will be exponentially more effective for you.

Now, when I attempt to catch the cat, the first thing that I'm going to do is try to learn more about cats through questions, research, and asking people. I'll try to figure out what cats like. What don't they like? I don't want to do anything they don't like and everything they do like. Maybe it's what they like to eat, the toys they like, the things that catch their eye. Maybe it's a scent that they like.

Of those fifteen minutes, I have three or four to collect this data, and if I'm going to catch this cat, I have to be, do, and have what it likes. There are a couple of agents in the office who have cats. Thanks to me fostering those relationships, they told me all about cats, so now I know what to get.

Speaking Their Language

It's not about me. See, the golden rule says, "Do unto others as you would want done unto you," but in this business, we have the platinum rule. The platinum rule says, "Do unto others as they would want to be done unto them." So, you speak their language. In this case, you speak the cat's language.

So what do I do? I calmly approach the cat, similar to how you did. I kneel down. I find things around the office. I've got little gadgets that make little noises. I've got some catnip, a little bit of food, and a bowl of water. I get down to the cat's level. I'm speaking in a very calm, tranquil voice. I'm making all the right noises that I have asked cat lovers about. The cat is not scared or tired. It was not just chased down and thought it was going to be killed and cooked for dinner. Now, it sees somebody who understands it, somebody who has its best interests at heart.

Finally, out of curiosity, the cat comes out. It sees the catnip and notices that I'm not moving toward it. It sees me down on my knees, smells the food, catnip, and sees the water. It slowly approaches. The cat walks up to the water, drinks it, has a little of the food, takes a little nibble of the catnip, and jumps in my arms. With thirty seconds to spare, I'm petting the cat, and I am now the winner of one million dollars.

How do you think I feel at this point? Well, I'm ecstatic that I won the million dollars, but I'm also calm, cool, and collected. I wasn't angry or frustrated. I took the time to create a plan. I strategized and customized the plan for the client; in this case, the cat itself. I learned what the cat needed. I delivered it. I gave it a clear path to what to expect. I was able to see that the cat could trust me. The cat, just like a lead, jumped right into my arms and I got the million dollars.

Why Do They Need You?

There are a few things that we learned here. One, you have to plan. You have to have a positive mindset, be devoid of any emotion, and execute your plan. The second thing to remember is that no deals, listings, clients, nor any two transactions are identical. The markets are constantly fluctuating and so are property styles and values. Client personality and preferences are changing.

For example, if you were to eat a bowl of cereal, would you use a fork or spoon? If you were eating sushi, would you use a knife, or would you use chopsticks? If you're eating a steak, would you use a fork and knife or just a spoon? You have to customize your approach to that client based 100 percent on their needs. Your first phone call to them will be the needs analysis. You're trying to find out why this opportunity is there. Why do they need you?

I call this "pain vs. pleasure." We're either adding pleasure to a goal that the client can't do on their own, or we are preventing the pain of something that could happen in the future if they don't make this transaction. One of the two is going to happen. People will pay 3-6 percent or even 10 percent for those types of services. But when you sit down with your client, your approach for that listing should be solely based on them. If they're a bowl of ice cream, you need to bring a spoon. If they're a big old steak, you need to come to the house with a fork and knife. If they're a plate of sushi, you need to show up with some chopsticks.

That's how you do it. You don't treat every client the same while spewing about how great you are and all the things that you do for all your clients. That will only turn them away.

While you're talking, guess what they're doing. They're judging you. They're trying to figure out if what you're saying is true. It may also be helpful to know about the 7-38-55 principle, which states that 7 percent of communication is the words we speak. Tone takes up 38 percent, and 55 percent is body language. Just by understanding that, you're in much better shape.

Why Questions are Beautiful

As we're going to get into in the next few chapters, what you're going to do is listen—the "L" in T.A.L.K. You must learn every single thing about that client, and it starts with questions. The beautiful thing about questions is that your client—in this case your future client—has to listen to understand. If you're asking the right questions, even before they answer, they will know that you understand how to answer or that you *will* understand, that you're there for the right reasons. But that's only if you ask the right questions.

Your listing appointments are not a billboard of all the wonderful things you do. They are a list of specific and strategic questions that lead the conversation down a path of predictable answers to create a plan for your client. The opposite would be to throw every tool in the tool box at your prospect and saying what most agents only mindlessly regurgitate—about all the marketing they do, and all the technology and leverage their broker has, or how many years they've been doing real estate and blah, blah, blah.

There is an old saying, "Nobody cares how much you know until they know how much you care." That couldn't be any truer than in the real estate industry. You have to show clarity in the process. You have to show trust in yourself that you can handle it. Then you have to create certainty that you are the best person for the job. Doing that will deliver clarity in your process, and trust between you and your client. They will say yes 100 percent of the time.

So, don't overcomplicate your appointments. Give clarity in the process and what you're trying to do for them. Build trust by asking the right questions and understanding their needs, and give them the confidence to make a decision and commit to you. You do that with communication in general—partly with the words you say, your tone, and how you present yourself in a way that shows you are the person for the job. If you look raggedy and sloppy, unshaven, or poorly dressed, you are a reflection of what you are trying to sell. That's all-important (at least 55 percent of the importance).

MASTERY DEFINED AS S + C / ECF × (DE) = BE

The Formula for Success Through Great Communication

Let's start by explaining what that formula means. The S is for "systems." You must have a consistent system for getting consistent results from your clients and business. Whether that be your daily system for yourself, in your mindset, your daily actions at your job—that system—or the system when you're approaching your client.

We have a system when we meet sellers. We have one when we meet buyers too. There's also one for when we meet investors. We have a system when we talk to "for sale by owners." And there's a system for when people reach out to us after having tried to sell their home themselves and could not.

There is a standard system, which also means—especially in real estate—that your listings all use a similar framework and have predictable results. When you don't get those results, you can analyze why. Having a system is huge, so find and master the process that works best for you and your type of clients, and then write it down and apply it daily.

Now, the C in this equation is "culture." You can have the best system in the world, but if you don't create a culture around the people, meaning a good mindset wrapped around core values, it will fail. Consider why we are all here. What is the goal of the organization or company? What do we believe in? Why do we do this and not something else? Why do we get up every day and put ourselves through this to do what we do? That's the culture. Who are you trying to be to achieve your goals? Do you want to build a purpose-driven organization?

You have to establish a culture with many different facets—vision statement, mission statement, daily goals, weekly, monthly, yearly, career goals, and weekly one-to-ones with staff and your clients. You must have a good culture. If there's no theme, there's no consistency in all the members of your team, or even in the way you might communicate from one deal to another. Master the culture, accompany it with a system, and then you're about halfway there.

Extreme Client Focus

The next part of the equation, ECF, stands for "extreme client focus." Any decision you make throughout the day should be in the sole purpose of benefitting that client. It's always about the client—extreme client focus. What do they want? What do they need? What are they afraid of? What are they happy or sad about? When's the last time you talked to them, and what might they be thinking now?

It's all about them. In fact, when we put our listings on the board, we don't actually use the addresses, just the names. I'm terrible with addresses. I rarely remember them, but I'd rather forget the address than the person's name. It's all about the people. They call this industry real estate, but if you're going to make anything of it, you're going to realize that it's actually a service by people and for people. Extreme client focus is a *big why*. That's also what creates the culture and how you come up with your system in the first place! It's what allows us to keep evolving and expanding those things over time for exponential growth.

Now, in any equation (as in this one), which variable has the most value? The answer is the (DE)—the multiplier. So while we're just adding systems and cultures, then dividing those into and extreme client focus, none of that is as effective as it could be if you didn't have the (DE) multiplier, which is "daily execution." We are creatures of habit. No single good deed is going to accomplish anything for us long-term. It's the slow, daily process of coming into your office, focusing on who your hot clients are, your warm ones, and your leads. Then you're just buying into that culture, developing the attitude and mindset, and focusing on your system and daily practices.

This has to be done every day. The BE stands for "business excellence." When you take a system, add a culture, and share that with every client as a source for all their decision making—and do that every day—you get *business excellence*. To sum it all up, C+S/ECF(DE) = BE means culture, plus systems, divided into extreme client focus, times daily execution, equals business excellence. That is the formula for growth in any market or economic climate.

Mastery is the Goal

As you grow in this, you have to remember that education is a lifelong goal. You're always going to want to learn more and get better at what you do. The key is to remember and know that the teacher is the best student. When you teach once, you learn twice. Mastery is the goal, so I suggest always freely sharing what you know.

Mastery, they say, is anything you've done ten thousand times. It's something you can do in your sleep. A lot of people don't have the vigor to keep at something they already know like the back of their hand. Others won't want to do anything for a long period of time if they're not great at it right from the start. They get immediately discouraged right away—"Well, I don't want to keep practicing something I'm not good at." Do you see the dilemma here?

This is the kryptonite of success and it keeps us from growing. I say start doing something, be uncomfortable. Do it even when you can't. Keep doing it when you can do it well. Keep doing it when you can do it excellently, and then realize that mastery means that you know you're not the potter. You're the clay. You are the one being molded, so as you get better, so will your actions. You will find new ways to get even better, more effective, and more efficient as you grow.

Get into those habitual tasks that might seem mundane and redundant, but over time, mastery will allow you to do things instinctively. When we watch people do amazing things in the Olympics, they can do that because they've done it so many times that they don't even have to think about it. What we don't see are the 10,000 times they worked at it.

Bringing Home the Gold

In real estate, it all starts with the famous listing appointment. You already know that we don't bring a ton of information or anything we've used over and over again with different clients to present. We come with information specific to that client's needs based on the phone call we took previous to that meeting.

Most everyone knows what a prequalifying telephone call is. That's in thousands of books around the world. That's not what we are teaching here, this book is all about the *why*. The why is the reason you're going to start doing all this stuff. The key is to have the right questions—strategic questions that give you the answers you seek, but tells the story of the process and builds trust in the benefits of working with you. Again, I'm going to read off some of them, but you want to customize it based on the needs of the clients. Luckily, it can easily be broken up into categories.

To Affinity and Beyond

In the initial consultation, the moment you walk in the door, you identify that you're early—it does matter. You wait by the door until you're invited in. Then thank them for the invite and remember to wipe your feet. Those details seem weird, but if they're not mentioned, they don't get done. Those kinds of niceties are perceived by your client before you say one word. That's important in communication. I call it "the language without words."

The connection that is made is defined as affinity. It's an energy that allows somebody to know that they can let their guard down and be comfortable with this person. All of that is highly important. The next step is to gather the specific information you know you will need. Designing those specific questions as you prepared for this meeting makes this part much easier and more effective. First, you need to know that you're in charge of the process, but they make the decisions. What you don't want to do is walk in and wait for them to tell you where to go like a scared cat.

After showing your gratitude by thanking them, you take the lead by politely explaining how the first thing they're going to do is walk you through the home and explain two things: What they loved about the home and what features would cause them to buy this home over another. You're also going to find out what they've updated since they purchased the home, or at least in the last few years. You also need to find out what they want to do to make it even better if they were to stay. You could even ask them, "On a scale of one to ten, how would you rate the current condition of your home?"

If they tell you seven, you say, "Well, it's not a ten. So, what are a few things that you would want to do to your house to make it a ten?" Their answers will tell you a lot. It's going to tell you the truth about what they feel about their house, and it's going to identify to you what possibly needs to be done from the eyes of a future buyer. This information can also help in the future during contract negotiations and even help to overcome objections about the home's list price.

From there, recall the F.R.O.G. concept I shared with you earlier: family, recreation, occupation, and goals. Why are you here (the agent)? What do you want to do (the client)? Where do you see yourself in five years, ten years, or even one year from now? Once you've asked about their family, their recreations, occupations, and goals, you know what is most important to them, and have thus swallowed the proverbial F.R.O.G. As an icebreaker, you're now going talk about whoever referred you. Over 75 percent of our business should be referrals or repeat business. If it's not a referral, you can still get into how they found you. Was it a mailer or another listing, or anything else? I like to find out how they know our mutual friend. How long have they known them? At the very least, it is good to know how they chose to call you.

Get That Big Why

When you find that common ground, right away, their guard drops, allowing you to paint a picture of clarity and start developing trust. From there, you're going to start with their big why, and while it is best to start with why, that doesn't mean asking "why" is always a good thing. Now, if there is a problem such as someone being upset during negotiations, "Why?" is a terrible question to ask. It's assuming that person is incorrect in feeling that way, which could make them feel invalidated. However, it's definitely one of the most important questions you can ask when you first get there.

"Why are you selling your home? Why am I sitting here?" Am I here to solve a problem or am I here to add joy to a goal? Is it pain or pleasure? Once you get that big why, then that's going to tell you so much and give you so many answers to questions you might not have asked yourself yet, or even thought to ask the client. It gives you the big picture.

If their answer is short and sweet, follow it up with, "Well, that sounds interesting! Tell me more about that." You want to know more. Never respond to a comment from your client with a one-word response, like, "Oh, awesome!" or "Cool," or even "That sounds great." You use the information given to you from your previous question to lead into another question. The deeper you can go with the why, the more real answers you'll get and the better you can serve that client.

Again, you want to repeat, "What is your goal? What do you think your greatest need is? How do you see the perfect timeline to make all this happen? What is most important to you—when you move, or how much you get? Maybe where you're going?" How about, "What are some specific questions or concerns you may have?"

Questions are the *best way* to connect to a client.

"Have you sold any houses before? What kind of experiences did you have? Do you have any fears that you're worried about?"

You've really got to get down to the big why. You've got to get the needs analysis so you can know what they're thinking, their expectations, and fears. This will help you deliver what is most important to them, give you a standard of service the client expects that you can exceed, and what events in past transactions the client wishes to avoid.

Set Your Plan of Action

Next is your plan of action. I call mine the seven P's. They're listing and marketing strategies. It's a proprietary system that I will be teaching in my classes because it works so well, but you can use any system you want. Depending on the market you're in, or what industry, your action plan will vary. You may not want, or have, to do the seven things that I do. But you need a differentiating factor. You must have something you can proclaim that you're doing that is unique and effective. So, use the principles in this book and the specific action plans that work for your type of client.

However, you should be concise and succinct when you are delivering the action plan. The main focus should be on them. You don't want to bore anyone with how great you are, but you need at least five to ten minutes to tell them proactive things you're going to do. If you are an agent worth half your weight in salt, you will have that information. Your broker is probably going to have it too, as a lot of brokerages provide that.

At that point, I detail my strategy. You would then have them repeat what they did to update the home, and what they would want to do if they were not selling. Make sure to get the age of what we call the vital few: the roof, the HVAC system, and the water heater. These are the normal functionalities of a home. Everybody wants constant warm, clean water. Everybody needs electricity, and they want the roof over their head to be secure, especially since they're not cheap to replace. You also want to make a note of anything that's defective—anything that's broken or not working, and what they plan on doing to fix it.

Then, of course, you get into the preparation of the home. Now, anything will sell. A two-by-four has value. A house is made of many two-by-fours. Heck, a cinder block has value, and a house has many of those too. Depending on the needs analysis of the client, they may want to do something different to get more money than what fair market value will give them for the current condition, state, and updates that apply to the home.

Customize the Plan

Next, you create a plan based on what needs to be done and their needs analysis. It's a combination of what to do, buy, fix, or enhance to achieve the goal.

Now, if they don't want to do any of that—they have no money and just want to sell—well, we have services for that too, otherwise known as "*as-is*," but that doesn't mean you do nothing. You clean that thing until it's spit-shined and you can perform open-heart surgery on it. Then you present it using the most professional photos, and you market it the best way, through your huge database and the IDX (Internet Data Exchange) of the worldwide web from pole to pole. You try to get top dollar by listing it within market value and trying to create an auction effect. This gets you a little market influence to help you at that price, and the rest should take care of itself because as markets shift and economic climates change, so should your plan as well as your adjustments. That is a small example of tweaking a strategy based on the different needs of a client.

Let's say that your client has had a rental property for ten years and wants to unload it at the height of the market, but it's been beaten up by a tenant. If this person has been collecting income for the last ten years, you're probably going to work out a strategy to update the home. The market is saturated with overpriced, underdone homes. This person has a decent cash flow to update it, and it's been rented for ten years, so it already has a stigma attached to it.

Now, let's look at the competition. Let's see where people are putting their money as far as houses under contract and how your competition looks regarding active listings—and we do better than them. We pull out the statistics, the odds of selling the home, and who you have to be better than to get exposure and get a contract, and then we execute it.

The next step is agreeing on the list price, dates, terms, inclusions, exclusions, and commission. 99.9 percent of agents bring all their paperwork to the listing appointment and have that client sign everything before they leave. I am one of the 0.1 percent of agents who do not. I feel that monotonous paperwork is not a value-added advantage for the client. A client could change their mind overnight. You're gaining nothing by having a client sign a listing agreement unless you don't have enough to truly offer to keep them as clients. If you earn their business the paperwork is the least important factor in the end. They're going to need to choose you wholeheartedly to move forward, and you will know that before you leave. When you can get started is really the last question.

Then the rest of this can be done electronically, and they can sign the listing agreement in five minutes. The main thing is to go over and have identified before you leave are the five main parts of the listing agreement: the list price, dates, terms (any kind of home warranty stuff that was going to be included, or out-of-the-ordinary statistical info), then of course, inclusions and exclusions. These are the things, like personal property, that won't typically be removed from a property, like a dishwasher.

You have to know those things, because they're not common knowledge, and sometimes people just want to take what they want to take. But you have to identify these things. Then, of course, the commission—what are you going to charge to do the job and why—and where's the value.

The Final Question for the Easy Close

The easy close—and I hate to call it a close because I'm not a salesperson—is the final question you need to ask: "Mr. or Mrs. Seller, when would you like me to get started?"

Now, at this point, you've laid out in your mind and understand the physical nature of the house. This includes what shape it's in, including defects and upgrades. You know all about their family, what they do for fun, their occupations, and their goals—the big why. You have a full-blown needs analysis. They know how you're going to do it. You're in full agreement about the list price, dates, terms, inclusions, exclusions of the content of the contract or listing agreement, and of course, the commission. Now, the only thing to decide is when to start. There's where you'll get your yes or no, and where you will know you got the job.

Then, before you leave, you create a mock timeline to iron out all of the different listing stages. The timeline will start with what we call the premarketing time period; next are the professional photos, so plan when those will be shot and marketed; then the day you actually list on the market; the grand opening that we do that first weekend of the listing; being active on the market; when the open house will be; and when you can expect to get the contract. Then, once you start talking about contracts, you must decide between "as-is" contracts and standard contracts. Lastly, be sure to remind them that later you will be sending them the three-page listing agreement you already discussed to sign.

It's hugely important that your clients and you understand, line for line, what those contracts mean and the differences between them. That could make or break a deal. The contract is where great success happens, but also great tragedy. So, master your contracts. Master your system, your culture, and your client focus. Do it every single day and you will have *business excellence*.

15

TALK IS
CHEAP

Take Action Every Day to Meet Your Goals

As we've seen, there's a lot of value in T.A.L.K. However, it is much more than simply talking! "Talk is cheap," as they say. The most important factor in all of this is action—physical action. There's an old saying I once heard: "There are a million ways to succeed in life, but there is only one way to fail, and that is by standing still." You could have all the ideas in the world, all the ambition, and all the brains, but if there's no action, nothing gets done.

Up until now, this book has mainly been about concepts, ideas, and mindsets—more disciplinary actions—but this is more of the process. In the previous chapter, we went over an example appointment for a listing agreement. However, these are day-to-day physical actions that we call the "I time," time devoted to yourself and your goals to become a better person tomorrow than you are today. It's the art of multiplying your value. Wheat grain can be ground and made into flour for bread to eat for a day, or it can be replanted and multiplied into one hundred stalks. It also has been said that if we commit to increasing our knowledge, skills, and capacity by one percent every day, in one year, we will have become 3,770 percent better than when we started.

These are what we also call "the 20 percent" from Pareto's 80/20 principle, which states that 80 percent of any effect comes from 20 percent of what caused it. In other words, 20 percent of what we do all day creates 80 percent of the results we see from those daily efforts. They are the 20 percent actions, and of course, they still start with the number one action, your morning ritual. The morning ritual is ultra-important and can never be broken. We mustn't halt it or replace it with anything else, because our morning ritual is the beginning of everything. That being said, when you identify what your 20 percent actions are, work on increasing those, and the 80 percent effect they will have on your life will increase exponentially.

Win the Morning, Win the Day

Your next step is to show up! Show up for work early every single day—no questions asked (unless you have business appointments). You would be surprised how many people in my office—and there are over a hundred—actually show up. The answer is—less than I can count on one hand. I get there at 8:30 a.m. every morning with the goal to be the first to arrive and the last to leave even before the handful that do show up.

Crazy, huh? But it's the truth. I happen to be in the top one percent in sales for the entire company natuonwide, *and* I'm also in the top one percent of those who show up early every day to work. That's no coincidence. So show up early every day!

Again, you're doing all this to program your subconscious mind. The body gets used to this type of repetition, and then you get more effective and efficient.

Put It in Writing

Regarding step three, get ready to make twenty-five written affirmations. For example, when I get to work, the first think I do is write down an affirmation I want to focus on, like, "I love getting four new listings a month." I jot that down twenty-five times. Years ago, some of you may have been punished in school. What did the teacher do? They likely made you write, "I promise I won't speak out in class," on the chalkboard ten to fifteen times.

There's a method to that madness. There's a reality that sets into the subconscious—the reticular activating system—that has to make sense of that phrase. It has to justify why you're saying and writing it; it has to do something about it. You can't lie to yourself forever. It might be a lie at first, but eventually, it will not be a lie. Your body will not allow it. The body holds the sense of everything you say. Anything you repeat over and over will become fact to you.

The upshot of this step is completing twenty-five written affirmations, followed by two strategically handwritten notes. First, go for perfect handwriting. Write slowly and intentionally. Use blue ink and avoid words like "me," "I," or "my" after the first sentence. Be very complimentary. Speak with purpose. Infuse it with gratitude. Be thankful for the fact you did a deal with them, that you even know them, and what they mean to you. These could be just random people you know or past clients.

The first thing to do upon arriving at the office is to send out two handwritten cards per day, every day. If you don't have 500 people to write a card to in a year (two people a day), you need to revert to the lead gen that we talked about earlier in the book. We'll continue to talk about it in this chapter to make sure you know. It could be your mother, another family member, your neighbor, a vendor you've done business with, and of course people you meet daily. Your first goal is to increase your database to 500 strong. Trust me when I tell you that it's easier than you think. This has to be done every day, Monday through Friday, fifty weeks a year.

You're Getting Warmer

The fourth thing you have to do every day is to examine your "warm list." A warm list compiles leads with the potential to be a sure thing. They are somewhere between a lead and what we call a "qualified warm lead." The warm leads are people who might be selling or buying within the next three to six months. If they're found through social media, random interactions, or what we call "live interviews," there's a good chance they might buy or sell. So really focus on your warm list, and always be on the lookout for new opportunities to add to it.

Next comes the eight-by-eight, which is eight touches—eight ways of reaching out to somebody—within eight weeks, to create a situation that allows you to get a deal, a referral, or build a relationship that increases the amount of resources you can offer to your clients. For instance, if your friend owns a pool company and a lot of your clients need pool service, maybe by approaching a client on your warm list—if there is no ability to create a transaction or get a referral—you could benefit that person by referring business to them. That builds a professional relationship that ultimately turns into a referral or a business transaction in time.

Helping people and spending time with them is never a waste. You build a relationship; you add value. You give, and the Law of Reciprocity gives back. But you've got to look at that "warm list" every single day because that is where everything starts as far as the transactions, as there are certain things you have to do to make money, and intentional focus is very effective. The largest gap between a warm lead and a new client is getting an appointment.

Once you have the appointment, your goal is to find their need and convey the solution to get an agreement for the job. The most important factor in getting agreements is to present ourselves and our process to buyers and sellers. Then we must show houses or market our homes that we have listed for our clients. If we're doing that, then the next most important thing is to write and negotiate contracts. Some of what we do is about protecting our clients' interests and equity in their home and negotiating on their behalf, but mostly, it's about the money. Yes, the selling of the real estate is for the client, but they're ultimately trying to make the most money possible.

The next thing to realize is that we're going to be assisting in the contract process itself: "What is your big goal, Mr. Seller or Mrs. Seller, or Mr. Buyer or Mrs. Buyer? We're going to help you along the way to get to that closing table and get into that dream home. Or finally sell your house after all these years. The kids have moved out and you're just going to fulfill a dream. That's what we're here for."

Then, of course—especially if you're a team lead—you want to manage your money and assets. Real estate has an ebb and flow of feast or famine. Even in nature, those honeybees—they're enduring famine eight months out of the year. They're eating flowers and sucking up pollen and making honey like crazy. The honeycombs exist because flowers won't be around all year. It's the same philosophy here.

Now You are Sizzling Hot . . .

Now we come to the "hot list." This is where some other fun stuff begins with active real estate clients doing things—like presenting to buyers and sellers, showing homes, promoting your listings, writing contracts, negotiating, and assisting your clients from contract to close.

Hot-list clients have literally looked you in the eye, spoken openly with you, shook your hand, and stated, "I want you to help me in real estate, and I'm ready to get started." This list is really where the money comes from. These are the active people you're working with, and you need to focus on them, they represent your 20 percent of Pareto's 80/20. Do you need to call them today for this? What happened last time? What's the progress? What is your next *proactive* action?

I always tell my selling clients, "I will be communicating back to you in two different ways." How often, we'll decide as well, but I'm either going to tell you the reaction from another agent or buyer regarding our recent actions (showings, open house, etc.) or what my own "proactive action" has been with your listing and what we've done to create interested buyers. Either way, communication of any sort of action has to be conveyed. A lot of the time, that's where agents drop the ball.

Other agents say, "You know what, if there were any interest from a buyer for your house, the buyer's agent would call me." That may be true, but waiting for a buyer and their agent to find and sell your listing for you is *not* how you are supposed to do your job as a listing agent. They may stumble across another house and forget about your client's house let alone go back to take a second look. We must be proactive and take the necessary steps to prepare the home for sale, price it right for the market, and present it to a buyer. You can't simply place a listing on the internet and pray that a buyer will appear. There's so much more that goes into it. So, if your phone isn't ringing, you should start dialing. Even feedback or weekly marketing strategies would be music to the seller's ear, even if you had no offers. Talk to your clients every week!

Giving Your Clients a "Good T.A.L.K."

The next thing you're going to do is make service calls to your clients. It depends on how many people you're typically working with, but you want to talk to your clients weekly, even if you're making daily calls to your various clients. But never go more than a week without calling a client, especially if absolutely nothing has happened for them. For buyers, maybe there is no new inventory on the market, so there are no houses to show. Or you have a listing with no showings, and nobody has called you with any interest. That doesn't mean you can skip talking to your client for a week. Call them.

Maybe say, "How do you feel? Do you have any concerns? Is there anything that you might be interested in talking about as far as tactics for marketing, or a future open house? Have you considered a price reduction?" Sometimes, it's nothing more than using our mouths to be an ear for our clients.

But reach out to your client.

"Mr. and Mrs. Seller, here are my thoughts—this is what I see happening in the market and here are some good options. Which direction would you like to go?"

Prepare before you call, but *call your client.* Never let a week go by. If it's been seven days and you haven't spoken to your client, you're losing. So, let's say you don't have any active clients yet. How and where do you get started if you have been in sales for a while, but in a slump? How can you get started?

No Cold Calls . . .

There are also three other types of calls in real estate: "review calls," "one-to-tens," or "chosen one" calls. For each of these three options, it depends where you are in your career. If you've been doing real estate for decades, you're probably going to stick with "review calls" and contact your clients based on their purchase anniversary. The review call is for an analysis—similar to a live interview—using the acronym of F.R.O.G. (family, recreation, occupation, and goals). Then you give an updated market review of what the house was worth when they bought it, what it's worth now, information on what else sold in the neighborhood since then, and how much it sold for. Then give them any specifics that they're interested in learning.

You get all that from your initial review call. However, a review works better in person. I have my assistant call to set up the review, and then I call to follow up to confirm when it will be. Then, of course, I do a live presentation in front of them at their home or a local coffee shop.

Turning Warm Leads into Hot Leads

If you are having trouble with clients on the fence, then you can do what I like to call the "one to ten" calls or conversations. This is when you contact someone who is a prospect or potential lead, but—for whatever reason they think—they're not ready to buy. Then we assign them a number based on which obstacles they need to overcome, or what questions must be answered before they're ready to see a house or sign a contract most of the time. If they're not ready and you don't know what to do next, you may wait for the client to figure it out and hope they call you back. That may work, and it sometimes does, but it's the least effective way to turn warm and hot leads into active clients. It is also an easy way to lose a client.

115

So the "one to ten scale" specifically is a proactive way of reaching out and helping your client get from where they are to where they want to be "ready to buy or sell." For example, maybe you are talking with a new client who is looking to buy, and he's telling you a big story. By the end of this thirty-minute conversation about all the obstacles in his way, if you have nothing more than empathy, you are not doing him or you any favors. We need to be the professionals and help guide them to where they want to be. If they tell me that they want to be in their dream home in six-to-nine months, then it's my job to help them get there.

So, my next question is, "Talk to me about why you don't think you can do it, or why you're not ready? If you were ready right now, would you want to buy a home?" If the answer is yes, then that's a great candidate for a "one to ten." Now, let's assume that ten things need to be done to buy a house, and each thing must be handled before the client is ready and willing.

"Tell me, John or Jane Doe, what is it that needs to be done?"

"Well, I need to talk to a lender and see where I stand, have them run my credit and get all the information of my taxes and my job. Then I need to talk to my employer because I was supposed to be getting a raise, and I know that's going to be huge factor. I wouldn't want to commit to buying a home if I wasn't getting that raise."

It could be something like that, but it's not something you blow off. You absorb it. You think about it. Our job is to find a solution, but you've got to keep it simple.

So you say, "Okay, Mr. Buyer, Mrs. Buyer, here's what we're going to do. I'm going to help you. Those sound like really easy things to overcome, and we're going to take care of them one at a time. I heard six things that we need to find answers to before we get started. That makes your one-to-ten number a four and the goal is to get you to a ten. As we overcome each obstacle, your number increases. Start planning for all, but start with the easiest. Talk to me about what your concerns are about the dogs, and let's get to the bottom of that." As you're talking about a few different things, you realize that the dogs need shots or medical attention—maybe doggy daycare. So, you call them up in a few days with some veterinarians and doggy daycare places—all sorts of things that solve that problem.

They say, "Thank you so much! We'll call them." Then you call them in a week. That problem is solved, and they say, "Thank you so much!"

"Now let's go to your other obstacles—the other concerns that you have. Okay, you need to talk to your boss. Let's focus on that now. When do you see your boss again? When do you go into work? What is it that you're worried about when talking to your boss? Is there anything that makes you think you might not get that raise? How much time needs to go by before you get the raise? Is there anything specific you have to do to get it?"

You paint a picture. Even if you know nothing about that part of the process, you get them thinking about how to solve that problem. Now you say, "Try that. If you have any issues, give me a call. Either way, I'm going to call you next week." At this point, they are a five and headed to a six. You call next week. "Hey, Mr. and Mrs. Buyer, how'd it go with the job?"

"Oh my gosh! We got the raise! It's done and it kicks in two weeks from now."

"Perfect! Now we've got to get you to that lender. We're going to start looking at properties. I know you don't want a condo, and that issue with the dogs is totally squashed, so you're good. Now that you have the raise, let's talk to a really good lender and see how that could really benefit you, and what our time frame is. I'm going to send you to a few lenders. They're all great ones we've worked with before. They're rock stars in what they do—pick the one that's your favorite." At this point, the client's number is a solid seven.

Within three weeks, you've taken a client from your warm list to being almost ready to go. You've given them attention. You've created a level of importance in their mind, and you've sped up the process. You didn't sit back for a few months and wait for them to call you while the market totally passed them by and interest rates became way too high and now they can't buy. You've been the agent that you should be, and now they're ready. The "one to ten" calls help you in that. They're all about guiding them to the point at which they will list their home or be ready to look at some. Now, the lender has checked the last three boxes for the buyer, and your client feels very accomplished (thanks to you), and they are now a ten.

The "Chosen One" Call

The third type of call, outside of "one to tens" and "reviews," is the "chosen one." These go out to people you've met before and are almost friends with, but they're currently acquaintances. You might have been better friends in the past, but not these days even if everything is good. You just need to rekindle the relationship. Those are the best. I tell new agents to look in their phones and email accounts for these types of people. The chosen one calls are the absolute best place for new agents to start! Maybe you've already done business transactions with them through another industry, or perhaps you went to school together. Either way, these are people you already met who know who you are. Your goal is to find out if *you* are the chosen one.

The conversation goes something like this: "Hey Tim, how's it going? It's Robert Paolini with Berkshire Hathaway. How have you been?" My next favorite thing to say is, "Is now a bad time to talk?" Always say it that way—not, "Is now a good time to talk?" You're being presumptuous by asking if it's a good time to talk. When you call somebody out of the blue, you should assume it is a bad time—not presume that it's good. At the very least, you are grateful they stopped what they were doing or thinking to answer the phone. Give them that opportunity to say, "Yes, call me back later." Most likely, though, they will say, "No, now is not a bad time to talk."

Then you reply, "Great! Thank you, I only want a few minutes. I've just been thinking about you recently and I just wanted to chat." That's when you follow the F.R.O.G. It sounds methodical, almost like a script, especially since it has its own acronym. But it's by far the best way to communicate with a professional in the least amount of time, and it is not a script; this is just an example.

You're talking about the four main things that every human being cares about. We've talked about this before. Who wouldn't want to talk about their family, what they do for fun, what they do for a living, and what they want to do in the future? That's everything to everyone.

After going through that, you're going to write down a connection between all of those things and how you are involved in them. In other words, how you can help.

"Oh yeah, tell your wife that my wife said, 'Hello!' She remembers all the fun times when we were going here and there. Hope the kids are doing great. By the way"—here's where the "chosen one" comes into play—"you know we were just talking about real estate and what I do. I'm not one of those agents that, you know, gets upset if every one of my friends doesn't buy or sell their house with me. But just out of curiosity, if somebody you knew came up to you and said, 'Hey, Tim, I'm really thinking about selling my house. Who do you know that you can recommend to me to help me out?' If someone asked you that, Tim, who would you say?" Then you pause.

The key is that, at some point, it should really be the truth, and it's a shame if you take it personally. No matter what they say, your response is, "That is fantastic! They're an awesome real estate agent." You can even add, "How do you know them?" They'll tell you. You just listen with an open mind. You're not judging.

Your tone is very positive, even more positive than before. But more often than not, the name that you hear will be yours, but if it's not, it doesn't matter. "Good for them. They're a great real estate agent. How and why did you two become connected like that?" You're asking for no other reason than curiosity. In the end, you may find out that there really is no good reason why they're together. In some cases—and in a lot of cases for us—there's still room for you to be "the chosen one." But you must ask it this way.

And if they say, "Well, hey, it'd be you, Robert. We love you to death. But no one has ever come up to us, which is why we haven't referred you." Well that is awesome news. I don't mean you're saying out loud to him or her, "That's awesome news." I mean literally, that's awesome news. Now, that warm lead—that random call that you made—becomes a hot lead or remains warm, depending on how well you know them or how serious they were about buying or selling, or what the time frame was. Remember, your call was random and your question was hypothetical. Your friend is not actually looking to buy or sell just yet, but the seed has been planted, and soon, you will get the call that you are the chosen one! Your old friend is now a future prospect and a channel to give and receive referrals.

The Law of Attraction Kicks In

Now it's time for the eight-by-eight, described earlier. You're now reaching out to them. All sorts of stuff is kicking in, most notably, the Law of Attraction. And it is going to say, "Look, you brought up a scenario. You added joy and value to another human being. You've made that other human being identify who you are and what you do. Now a little bit of that is stuck, for a short time, in their subconscious. So more than likely, an opportunity for a referral will manifest itself this coming week." Trust me.

Because again, the brain has to create a reality for the thought. This guy just had a great conversation with you. Now, he knows, or was reminded, that you're a real estate agent, and you've hinted at the business. You didn't ask for business, and he made you a promise.

Eventually, I promise you that someone's going to come up to him and say, "I need to sell my house." Now, he's going to say, "Call Robert." Cue theme music for *The Twilight Zone*! Right, I can't believe that happened. Well believe it, because that's exactly how it works.

People say that it's a coincidence or the power of suggestion. If he yawns, then she'll yawn. This is a real thing and I can't stress that enough. This is a perfect example and explanation of how "the chosen one" calls work.

Up Close and Personal: The Live Interview

The second-to-last thing you're going to do is a live interview. This is nothing more than another F.R.O.G. format. This conversation happens at either at a party, a get-together, a random call on the phone to one of your leads, past clients, or someone you know on social media. It could also be somebody you know well enough to feel comfortable talking to about their family, what they do for fun, what they do for a living, and what their goals are.

The key is to mention what you do. If you ask the right questions, they're going to give you the right answers and you'll be able to guide and steer the conversation. You're trying to discover what is most important to them or what they need and want most and find a way you can help them.

In a live interview, talk about other people's family, recreational activities, their job, and their goals—but then finish by talking about real estate. It would be better if the conversation about real estate answered questions that were part of what you ask them. At the very least, real estate has to come up. With live interviews, just like "the chosen one" calls, the "one-to-tens," and the "reviews," you're going to set up an eight-by-eight situation—eight weeks (basically two months of touches) and reaching out to someone in ways that puts you at the top of their mind and serves their needs.

Live interviews are very strategic, and they start with a call. This initial call is, of course, going to be the interview itself. You want to find out everything about that person. You want to know about the family, the wife, the children, everything. You want to load up on information and find a need. That's what the call is for—to find that need. That is also why it's called an "interview" and not just another conversation—you just asked questions and the other person does all the talking.

People never tell me "No," because I never ask unless I know I'm solving a problem. If I'm having a conversation and the person's says, "I have no money, no rental properties, no nothing," my next question is *not* going to be, "Can I sell your house?" You *must* be there to help. It's not about trying to get what you want. The call is learning more about them, and I'll get to why a little later. Call from the perspective of love, not fear, and you will be amazed at all the ways you will find to help them. Through reciprocity, you have now planted seeds of future business and/or referrals.

Update Your Database

The last thing you're supposed to do every week is to update your database. Make sure your clients who are in it earn the right to stay. Make sure that they're answering your calls, active on your website, respond to your emails, and that they're grateful for some of the things you send them. You want to help people that want be helped and not everyone does.

If those people are on your social media and interact with you—they stay. If they're not, they are removed. You have to be disciplined with your database, especially if it's tiny. With databases, it's not quantity. It's all about quality. I can do more with two-hundred great leads, two-hundred terrific past clients, and a strong sphere of clients than I could with twenty-thousand local people in any given farm area. It's much more powerful to have a high-quality database you interact with.

So every week, you have to add and subtract people. This will keep you on pace with meeting other folks. Every day, get out into some of the social networks you're in, your neighborhood, or some of your kid's events, like sports and school. All that stuff keeps you constantly enhancing your database. When you're reaching out to random people, you're just trying to help them. If your neighbor is painting his fence or trying to change a lock, or whatever, you're there helping. But update that database.

So that's it, my friends. Talk is cheap. Action is where it's at, but the key is that if you do it every day and repeat it every week, there's no question you will reach 100 percent of your goals.

NEGOTIATING!

A Sales Pitch Starts with "Hello"—Negotiations Start with "Know" and "No" and "I Know"

I'd like to start this chapter on negotiating with my version of the definition. Negotiating is *nothing more than a series of empathetic, calibrated questions toward another for the purpose of seeking to understand that adversary's or counterpart's needs, wants, beliefs, leverage, and what we call the "black swan,"* which I will soon explain. Not one "know" sounds the same, right? When you hear the word no, it begins the need to negotiate. The first action we must take as negotiators is to learn all we can, all that we need to "know"!

A lot of this information is from a terrific book called *Never Split the Difference* by Chris Voss. Never splitting the difference seems to be unfair and anti-win-win, but in reality, it's not. Take for example:

> You get up in the morning, put on your suit, and then you try to decide whether to wear black or brown shoes. You want brown, and your wife wants black. If you split the difference and compromise, you're going to end up wearing two different colored shoes. That's not a win-win. It's a lose-lose. From purely a fashion sense, you have failed—plus, nobody got what they wanted. That's a simple example of why splitting the difference is a lazy way of negotiating.

The strategy of many agents would be to give a really low offer, and then start playing a game of halves back and forth until they come to a line in the sand. That strategy won't do anything for your career or clients. Don't worry—the negotiating you will learn in this chapter is very effective, but it is not aggressive, assertive, or rude in any way! It's all about a Good T.A.L.K. As you read, you'll learn an effective, simple, non-pushy way of negotiating. In fact, most of the time, your counterpart won't even know.

Listening, the Weapon of Choice in Negotiations

The first and most important thing to do, and the weapon of choice, happens to be one of the letters in our acronym T.A.L.K.—listening. Listening is your best weapon when negotiating—and for a lot of other things, too, but particularly when negotiating. Listening will fill you with all the information you could ever want, including things like that adversary's client's needs, wants, beliefs, leverage, and the "black swan"—just like in the definition.

The "black swan" is also from *Never Split the Difference*. This is crucial to the entire deal. It could be really beneficial or really detrimental. It's a major factor that neither party is aware of. Typically, the first one to find it wins, because this black swan gives you all the leverage. It's the secret element to the entire deal, and it's based on what one side of the transaction wants and the other side wants, added together. The goal is always to search for that missing link. It could easily satisfy both your needs and wants, as well as your client's. That is a true win-win, and it's far from splitting the difference.

The "black swan" helps you (as the seeker) come up with something of value for the client. The best part is that it does not always have to come at the heavy expense of your adversary. There are many ways for each side to get what they want without conceding anything. However, if leverage is required, it can also be found.

Kindness Counts

The only way to get pertinent information like this is to ask questions. That's why the definition started with a series of empathetic and calibrated questions. In many cases, emotions come into play, so it is important to remembver another major component of communication "kindness," another part of T.A.L.K. So, whenever you're negotiating, be kind. Strangely enough, most professionals are least kind when they're negotiating. But this is terrible because they can't hear what they need to hear to come up with a solution to the problem, nor does their adversary seek to understand. Then the things they say and the information they convey may be too much, too little, or come across as condescending and rude, and the other person simply puts up a wall. Kindness is absolutely paramount. Kindness opens the mind and heart to rational understanding.

It all starts with listening. Everybody who negotiates wants to be the first person to talk. Nobody wants to listen, and those who *are* listening are typically waiting to talk. They're almost not listening at all, and if they are, it's on a very low level. They're not retaining nor processing much of what they hear. Therefore, not a lot is getting done. You basically have two people talking over each other, and nobody is hearing what the other person is saying. They cherry pick what they want to hear and believe. Most deals get blown to pieces this way.

It doesn't matter if you're selling houses, pencil erasers, or bed pans—you have to listen, and the best time to do it is at the start of a conversation. In doing so, you're relinquishing the initial control to your adversary. However, that will disarm them. While they're talking, they're not listening or judging. They're just talking. A lot of the time, they're speaking without thinking about what they're saying. They're saying what's actually running through their mind, which most likely will be the truth. Their words will contain information that's important to you.

From their perspective, they feel they've got control. If you're not trying to squeeze a word in, and they're doing all the talking and conveying to you everything their client wants, needs, and demands, they're doing their job. To most real estate agents—or most professionals for that matter—negotiating is merely talking about what their client wants. Like I said before, a sales pitch is simply something that starts with a "hello." Negotiations start with a "no." If you don't hear a "no," you're actually not negotiating.

So listen, listen, listen. Be kind. Be smart. Look at it similar to blackjack. You only want to show one card. It's better than showing none and preferable to showing both. You want to tease them and pique their curiosity. The strategy of negotiations is much like blackjack.

An agent or salesperson will be regurgitating tons of valuable information about their client and you'll be listening for emotion. Of course, you're listening for those needs, wants, major concerns, and beliefs, too—that's important to know. Whether you agree or not at the moment, you can't be emotional. Just listen. You have to train yourself to listen and hear without bias.

Strategize Your Response

In most negotiations, and in most professions, you can't respond without conveying new information. A good excuse and reason to avoid this is to, at the end of that agent's or salesperson's rant, simply thank them for their time. Tell them that you have to speak to your client about what they want to do and what they think. That gives you time to strategize your response.

All this valuable information will allow you to add even more tangible or circumstantial information to the deal when you're doing your research. When you come back to the table and sit across from that adversary, you're going to win. It's over. They have no idea what's about to hit them. The good news is that they may not even realize and will most likely be happy with the result.

There are two words you're waiting to hear, and if you hear them, stop. You've done it. If your point is made, go in for the close. Those two words are "that's right." Not "you're right." That's different. They could be giving you a stubborn response and be throwing in the towel, not wanting to argue with you. But "that's right" means they understand what you are saying.

The only way to get them to say this is to start with the first of three core parts of negotiating: "labeling." Labeling is taking the emotion of your client and recognizing it verbally. They will know that you know how they feel. This will also verbally repeat vital information and how it relates to their client. You have not given a solution or opinion of your client, so you are simply confirming their feelings and why! An example of labeling in real estate would be an agent for a buyer conveying his or her buyer's concern that the seller's counter offer is too high to appraise. A labeling response shows not only that you are listening, but that you care. Your response might be, "Yes, I can understand why the buyer feels that way. Nobody wants to be forced to pay more for something than it is worth."

Thought: Mirroring—an Important Negotiation Strategy

There's another strategy called "mirroring." This is a great way to get the client to agree to what you want by simply repeating the last few words that they said in a sentence, or repeating the very end of a complete thought.

For example, if your adversary were to tell you that the buyer wants ten thousand dollars in seller concessions (money back at closing), you could fly off the handle and freak out. You could interrupt him with a "no" and relay what your client wants. But if you are a professional negotiator, you'll start with a mirror. Simply say, "Ten thousand dollars?" and pause.

The most crucial part of mirroring is the pause. Many people have tried to sell me something, and the moment they ask the question, they continue to talk without pausing or stopping. They're too afraid of my answer, so they just keep going. I couldn't say, "Yes," even if I wanted to. In this case, it is even more important that you pause. Your tone is very important as well. It should be without negative emotions and with a downward inflexion Chris Voss calls "late night radio voice."

Being bold in any negotiation is not about yelling as loudly as possible at your adversary. It's not about being stern because you care or don't care about the deal. It's about your ability to pause. It's extremely awkward, but it's something that you have to practice. It requires practice for mastery like anything else, but the pause is all-important.

So you simply say, "Ten thousand dollars?" and pause. Have you ever had someone say something to you but you couldn't quite hear them? So you ask them to repeat it, but as they do so, you begin to remember what you heard. But what you heard is different than what they're repeating. They're making it nicer, easier sounding, or making it more in your favor. They're adjusting it just a little bit to make sure it's not offensive, wrong, or too much. You're basically experiencing the principles of "mirroring."

Human beings live in the gap between subconscious and conscious. When you are mirrored, your reticular activating system has to make sense of it so you can believe and affirm what you just asked. If it doesn't, it's because there's something inside of you that *knows* what you said might be "BS" or not 100 percent the truth. So, what happens? Without your ability to control yourself, you adjust what you've said.

So now your adversary may have already been told that the client would agree to seven thousand dollars. So he tells you, "Ten thousand dollars," but it's not about bickering or splitting the difference. It's about negotiating. Then you say, "Ten thousand dollars?" That person doesn't have to be a rocket scientist to know there's something about ten thousand dollars that just doesn't work.

So they'll say something like, "Well, to be honest, the client said nothing less than eight thousand. They just won't take a penny less than that, but they wanted me to start at ten thousand." But you do it again, even multiple times, until it either doesn't make sense, or you start getting into incorrect labeling (which we'll get into), or you close.

So you mirror again and say, "Eight thousand dollars?" But not in a negative or insulting way—just repeat it: "Eight thousand dollars?" Now you must open your ears to hone in on what they say because then you have to push back the empathy to their side of the negotiation. You must make them see that you understand where they're coming from. You and your client are now in a position that isn't a "won't" or "shouldn't" mode, but a "can't" and a "must not" one. In the end, if $7,000 is their client's bottom line and your client's max, everybody wins.

Don't Say Won't

"Won't" is not good in a negotiation. It lets the adversary know that your client is choosing to go against them. However, if you instead frame it around a "can't"—whether it's a "won't" or not—they're much more receptive.

So, the adversary comes back and says, "Give me a break! Eight thousand dollars isn't good enough for your client? This isn't going to work. This deal's over."

"Well, I apologize. I am sorry. I do not want to offend anybody. Eight thousand dollars, if they were to agree to that, is an absolutely wonderful gesture. We appreciate it very much. I know my client would love to get just seven thousand dollars back in seller concessions. I apologize, but my client just *can't* do it. They're not in a position to move forward with this deal with only eight thousand in seller concessions. It has to be . . ."

Ten thousand dollars, seven thousand dollars—it doesn't matter. It all depends on what they're looking for. But you can label their offer as something that you understand and appreciate, but you're telling then "no" because of a circumstance of the seller. That goes right back to that adversary's reticular activating system, and now they have to make sense of that fact, with something that is conceivably circumstantial.

When they go back to their client—whether they realize it or not—they truly become your adversary. If your client is a buyer who wants ten thousand dollars in seller concessions, and the other party was trying to hustle us down to seven thousand, you'll most likely get the ten thousand dollars. If you're representing the seller, and the buyer wants ten thousand, the client will most likely get seven thousand negotiating this way.

But the beauty of negotiating this way is that it not only gives your client what they want, but it doesn't ruin or taint the emotion, affinity, or energy of the deal. Both parties don't despise each other, and together they can close. In fact, I have become friends with many of the agents I've done deals with even after tough negotiations.

After the initial contract, other real estate dealings come next, like inspections, appraisals, or trying to negotiate inclusions, exclusions, and personal property. All of these go so much better—even the closing itself—if you use kindness and professionalism as you negotiate with empathy and strategy.

It All Comes Back to Questions

From the start, questions are the key. There's no formula for the questions that you can use in each and every negotiation, but you'll know which ones to ask because you've done your due diligence and gleaned all you need to know about your client. As long as you know the necessary details, then all you have to do is think of all the questions that would collect that information without *directly* asking. Then you'll have all the strategic questions. You won't be fluffing, stuttering, tiptoeing, or beating around the bush. You'll be direct and professional, and you'll get exactly what you need to know when your calibrated questions (which is another part of the definition of negotiating) provide them with necessary information. It's always best to rehearse the negotiation before it happens. That way, you can strategize where and how the adversary may come back at you. Base your questions around guiding the conversation toward answers your client wants or ones that help to fill in the pieces to the puzzle that started with the word "no."

Then, last but not least, some questions won't be answered, and the agent won't convey certain things. In a lot of cases in real estate, it happens a lot when you're dealing with a "single agent" (somebody who has a fiduciary responsibility to their client) as opposed to a transaction broker who's there for the good of the deal. There are a lot of things that they're not obligated to tell you.

Be Wrong on Purpose

The way to get important information about another agent's client is by using a technique called "false labeling," which I mentioned earlier. It's like labeling (when you're identifying the emotion of the client based on the circumstance to let them know that you understand), but this time you're going to ask a question to see if that their answer matches the ones you expect. You also already know the question is invalid.

For example, a big motivating factor to sell would be a divorce. Nobody is looking for profit. Everybody's bitter. They want to sell fast, but they don't want to be taken advantage of. So, buyers love this information.

Let's say that you ask your adversary, "Hey, they getting a divorce? Kind of looks that way."

"No, no, no, no. They're not getting a divorce. They love life. They're fine," they say, as if everything's great. They might also say, "I can't comment on that."

But if you falsely label by making a statement that most likely is not true, they'll divulge something.

You say, "Ah! Okay, I get it. That makes sense now. They're getting a divorce. Now, I can see why they're saying this."

If it's important for you and for your client to know whether they're getting a divorce, and you don't know for sure, it's best to label it incorrectly. Then listen for the tone and tempo of what your adversary says. Almost every time, you'll know the truth within just a few seconds of false labeling since that person has to defend what you just said.

In some cases, they'll be honest with you and say, "Yeah they are. You got me." If they truly believe you have listened well enough, and you've identified a hidden secret through falsely labeling it, there is your black swan. They're getting a divorce. The home is in preforeclosure. They've got one mortgage at a bank-approved price. It's much lower than we thought.

Now you should shift gears toward helping your adversary's client solve a problem. Finalize the divorce, sell the house, and get it done. There could be a lot of other elements involved, but you have to strike at the heart and core of the biggest concern and the biggest "black swan" of your adversary. In this case, by falsely labeling, we've done both. We find the right price all parties agree on, and we begin allowing those sellers to feel they can now move on with their life.

And agents, make sure when you're bragging to your clients about how well you negotiate, you give them the definition and keep them in the *know*.

In the beginning, our job as real estate or other sales professionals is to find buyers for sellers, and sellers for buyers, but in the end, our job is to get the job done! Get it sold and achieve the goals your client has had from the beginning!

17

THE BIG
PICTURE

It's Not About What You Are Ready to Do, but What You Are Willing to Do

This is just the beginning. You are about to begin connecting principles of masterful communication that have limitless potential. However, the secret to a good T.A.L.K. isn't actually talking. It's *action*! Even the wheel wouldn't exist today had it been simply left to the imagination. You started this journey with all the ingredients for success, and now you will have the recipe.

Good T.A.L.K. Great Sales is more than a book. It is a coach, a mentor, a teacher, and an ongoing reference of unchanging principles that work in any market at any time. The book itself is a great tool, and it can be used to go back and reread parts you need for certain situations on a daily, weekly, and monthly basis.

If you've learned anything from this book, it's that good daily habits, practiced consistently, are the key to success of any kind, at any level. Now, fine-tuning and tweaking what you do will come naturally. You don't have to already know how to do it; you just have to start moving. You just have to act.

That reminds me of another comparison between the way human beings live and what the reality is. A lot of what we experience and feel is found in nature. It's found in the plants, the ground, and the sky around us, like growing, becoming better, and doing more—an overwhelming thought, isn't it?

People just think, "It's too much. I can't do this," or, "I can't see the whole journey from start to finish so it's just too much to handle." Think about something as simple as a towering oak tree. The only action that is required to create that is to literally drop a seed into the soil. Nature, God, the spirit—call it what you want—but as human beings on God's earth, we are not required to know how to handle everything. We don't create things. We don't make them grow. All we do is simply plant the seed.

The Secret to Success—Movement!

We are always moving, even if we are not going anywhere. Everyone is always trying to define success, but it has a billion different definitions. Failure has but one. Failure is nothing more than standing still or doing nothing (the opposite of movement). Great things take time. Instant gratification is a myth for success. Just do it, keep going, and never give up!

Always remember that movement is required, so don't take for granted those mundane tasks we go through every day. As we learned from the butterfly effect, one mundane task leads to another. Our minds and bodies have to justify everything we do and think.

If we change what we do and think about the good—the greater good of it all—then slowly but surely, we will shift our way of thinking. A journey of ten thousand steps starts in the mind because, to start moving, we must remove all doubts and start finding the answers to our questions.

Overcoming Obstacles As You Go

Another good lesson brought to the surface by this book is how to overcome problems. We are defined by the way we treat ourselves and others. That being said, controlling our emotions is a great way to sustain good communication even when bad things happen. Genuine kindness is hard to fake, but you can create it within. That simple principle is the best way to overcome problems in the professional world when other people are involved.

Happiness is found within. You'll see it on the faces of the kids of some of the poorest countries. But people's inability to overcome problems is what causes issues. Everybody starts their day wanting to be good.

Few people get out of bed thinking, "You know what, I want to cut people off and have a bad attitude and be rude to somebody today." Most people have good intentions, but they don't back their mental state with continual, consistent, and repetitive actions and rituals to activate their reticular activating system. Daily repetition is key for as long as it takes. You must begin to find a solution to the problem. If you feel that no problem is too big or too hard to overcome, then your attitude will automatically be better because you're not fearing or worried about them.

As was stated earlier in the book, babies and adults both cry—adults just cry over different things. It's always at a crisis point with no answer. We can't find a solution, mentally or physically. The only thing we can do is cry. Just as you grow from a baby to an adult, if you grow mentally, physically, and spiritually stronger, you can overcome those problems, and they don't affect you, nor does the thought of them.

A friend of mine once said, "When you want to make a change, start moving. If the journey becomes too difficult and your body begins to fail, call on the strength from your mind to continue moving forward with your body. If your mind starts to fail and your body begins to weaken, you summon the God-given spiritual part of your body—the core of you, the light inside of you."

I have learned that how far we go in life has less to do with what we can do and more to do with what we can take. When we accomplish more, it is not because we do more, but because we have *become* more. Raise your tolerance, temperance, and your capacity, and you will rise to a level that allows you to do, be, and have what you want. That also means if we are not what we want to be, do, and have, then it is more about us than anyone else. Start from within.

Honestly, it sounds like a cliché, but the truth is that we don't really "rise to the occasion." In my opinion, what we do is fall back to our highest level of preparation and mental capacity. We have to know that even if we don't have the answers, it's going to be okay, and that is the first step.

We all have temperaments. We all have fears and impulses. So when there's a stimulus around us, be it exciting, maddening, happy, or sad—especially things that upset us and make us angry—we typically react, but we don't necessarily have to.

The Five-Second Rule

To help with this, I created a five-second rule. When anything bad happens to you, go somewhere private and vent any way you would like to—yelling, screaming, writing, banging, whatever. But give yourself only five seconds to vent in any way that you want. Then, no matter what, you're not going to allow that emotion back into your thoughts about that problem.

Now, unfortunately, you will have to think about that problem again, but that does not mean you have to bring emotion into it. In fact, if you don't think about it again, you're really just running from your problems, and you don't need a book for that! You can guess what will happen if you run from your problems. But if you face them with an optimistic and positive perspective, the solution can and will be found.

Remember the five-second rule. Vent, scream, get it out. Unleash the physical part, but never let it back in. Be content with accepting what comes after that.

Believe it or not, this is difficult and takes a lot of practice. I've done it many times, but I have not had to do it in a very long time. I never feel any sort of emotional anger—just a brief, fight or flight response and nothing more. This type of emotional control keeps your feelings in your heart and not in your head, so it's much easier to dissipate and eliminate.

Words cannot describe the peace that comes over a person who has mastered the five-second rule. I am living proof. Whether I'm on the road; at the office; in a staff, manager, or broker meeting; or if catastrophic things happen to family and friends, the five-second rule helps to control the reaction.

The result is health, happiness, and inner peace. You're a better communicator. You're a better negotiator and problem solver. Because you're less stressed, you can help more people, and it increases the quality of your professional and personal life. It's an absolute must.

Instant Gratification is the Enemy of Success

Expectations are futuristic feelings usually reserved for fear or faith. Success of any type is a journey, and that journey begins by becoming the person you need to be to get started. Anything worth having should not be given to you the moment you think about it. Gratitude is felt when we are present in the now, and regret is dwelling on the past, so if we are to live as we are when we are not where we want to be, we must define our expectations and make sure we have faith to get there.

Instant gratification is the enemy of success, growth, and peace. To me, it's the archfoe of everything that our brains use to justify things that make us happy in our life.

I tell my kids, "When you eat candy, it's going to taste good going down and feel bad later. When you eat Brussels sprouts, it's going to taste bad going down but feel good later." That's nothing more than delayed gratification. They didn't get instant gratification from the sprouts, but they also didn't get rotten teeth and a stomachache. Again, even in an organic, nonpersonal way, you see the principles of delayed gratification.

What you've also learned from this book is that you must create connections with a potential client. To do this, there are three requirements. Remember, when you have that interaction with somebody and experience that "moment of truth," the ultimate goal is delayed gratification and a long-term professional relationship. The moment of truth is when you find yourself face-to-face, on the phone, or with a client and you're poised to create a future business opportunity for either party. Just remember that there are three things that you have to convey right away, or there's a reason, besides the timing not being right, that you won't get that client. You need clarity, trust, and flow, or "C.T.F."

"Clarity" means that the process, in and of itself, is understandable to the clients. "Trust" means that *you* are the right person for the job. "Flow" means that you are in a position to be chosen. In other words, that client may know ten other friends or family members who do exactly what you do, but if you're in the flow—and influencing them currently in their life—you will get the job. You could be helping them with their career, or with a personal thing, or even if it's a relationship based on a referral. That's flow. Flow is being relevant to somebody's current life. So, if there's nothing else that you can physically apply in your daily actions, remember to show clarity, trust, and flow with a client, and you will get that business every time.

C.T.F. is part of delayed gratification because, although there's daily effort involved, the results appear slowly. However, those who are in the know understand how effective and exponential the results can be if you have the time to wait. If you believe that you will get a deal from your first handshake, you may quit before you get started. It takes time.

You Can't Beat Face-to-Face and Eye-to-Eye

When beginning a career in selling, I would also suggest joining or creating a networking group. And I don't mean an online one, I mean offline. There are a million groups that you can already join on the internet, but they will only flood you with emails. We need to go back to the grassroots of human interaction. There are also many who say that if everyone is doing things one way, it would be wise of us to do the opposite. Be different and cut through the noise if you want to get people's attention.

No matter what technology is invented, nothing will be more impactful than face-to-face, chest-to-chest, eye-to-eye communication at arm's length, with the vibration of a good, old-fashioned handshake. That is a principle that will stand the test of time. Just like, "What goes up, must come down." A face-to-face will always win in effective communication.

Maybe you'll feel more comfortable on the phone or texting, but that does not mean it's more effective. That just means you're enabling your fears, inhibitions, or misconceptions. It's still all about face-to-face communication.

When you build long-term relationships, it's not about meeting a million people. It's about caring for a handful. This will embed you as a permanent relationship in that person's life, all their clients, and everyone who knows, likes, and trusts them, and is in their flow.

Networking groups are not easy to start, but they are worth it. It took many months to get our group from four people to about twenty, and another year to get another ten organically. We have since attracted like-minded members who were all good people and synergistic. We pass out so many referrals—it would dwarf a group twice the size, proving once again the power of quality over quantity. We also avoid cliques with people joining against others as well, which can not only hurt the quality of a group, but destroy it altogether. There's less baggage and negativity that can creep into any organization packed with adults.

You don't need a lot of members. Quantity does not matter, but quality does. It can be done; it's just all a matter of using the same principles that you would use to gain clients for yourself.

The 80/20 Principle

So far, moving forward has been about effectiveness and capacity, but how well we do the things we should do defines how productive we are. Since we all only have twenty-four hours in a day, where do some find the time, and where is the edge?

Remember the Pareto Principle from Chapter 15? It states that 80 percent of any effect comes from 20 percent of what caused it. Vilfredo Pareto was a local economist who developed the principle in the late 1800s while observing the economic state of his home town in Italy. The 80/20 principle can be found all around us, but it also lays the groundwork for what you should and shouldn't be doing throughout your day. Just know that 20 percent of what you do is responsible for 80 percent of what you give. In other words, 80 percent of the harvest you reap comes from 20 percent of the seeds you sow, which is remarkable.

That tells us that we need to find out what that 20 percent is and try to up it. Throughout your day, analyze what your most effective tasks are and increase them. People say, "Well, I don't really know what to do or how to do it." I've got good news for you.

Do not worry about what you are ready to do or what you can do. Look at what you are willing to do.

You've got to start somewhere. Just get going and watch the results happen. However, you will start to see more of what works just by doing more. You should also begin by analyzing your week broken down into what you normally do each hour of each day. Change will be required, but this should be subtle and enduring. People will push so hard to change, and then they become overwhelmed and totally give up. We all know quitters never win and winners never quit, but the key is consistency. You don't go until it's five in the evening, or go until you are tired, or hungry, you go until you are done or until you get there.

In the end, Pareto teaches us how and why to be conscious of our actions each day by leveraging our with results by prioritizing our daily tasks that produce the highest results for maximum production and effectiveness.

Extra Effort

Another great book I once read, *212 The Extra Degree* by Sam Parker, talks about the power of one degree (the metaphorical extra effort). It says:

> "211 degrees with get you scalding hot water, really hot water—as hot as you can possibly imagine, but it won't boil. 212 degrees however, will boil. With boiling water, you can move mountains."

With boiling water comes steam, and with steam comes pressure. Pressure can move a freight train, but I've added a little bit more to that story. Pressure is key (the steam is how you get it). The only thing you would get from boiling water that is not under pressure is steam. As soon as you put that power under pressure, you get your results.

It's the same with humans. When we are under pressure, we do better. With no pressure, no diamonds. I'm sure that you've heard that. That's another part of the problem-solving aspect that I started talking about at the beginning of this chapter. Just know that in the end, the struggle will make you better and more capable of handling problems. It also reminds us to keep growing and going until we reach our goal.

Pain or Suffering We get to Choose

In our lives, pain will always exist. Pain, as you may remember from Chapter 13, will manifest itself from the regret of failure, or it can exist from the effort required to gain what we want. One is self-induced and the other is a reaction to inaction. Now, getting what you want provides pleasure, but you will still feel the pain of the struggle and grind. But, if you have pleasure from doing whatever you want whenever you want, and you don't want to work hard, then you'll have the joy of having a leisurely life and making easy decisions. That, however, will leave you with the pain of regret, which is true suffering by living in a state of perpetual wanting.

That being said, pain is not a bad thing. In fact, it is required for growth and improvement, but the suffering part is optional. Many people are suffering, and they see it as pain. Therefore, it becomes exponentially harder for people in that state of mind to add more physical pain or action to their lives, especially if they don't believe those painful habits will have a positive effect. The big thing to understand is that the feeling of pain from inaction or guilt is not actually pain, it's suffering. If you can grasp that idea, you will start to see more value in pain and how your body and mind respond on a conscious and subconscious level whether you are aware of it or not.

Time for a Calculated Effort

Time and effort can be calculated to show the value of failure. Ostensibly, they're both the cause of failure, and this is simply the nature of this book. It was written to teach you how to do things that will change your life forever. That will help you be, do, and have anything you've ever wanted. But it's just information. It requires some application by the reader. To make this information do anything for you, you're going to have to put in *time* and *effort*.

You might be thinking right now that time and effort also bring success, but that would be false. Time and effort bring about potential success, and success happens if you excel at the quality and frequency of your time and effort.

Most of the time, people are not willing to commit to quality and frequency because they simply don't know how. The motivational, inspirational, and outside-the-box thinking that leads to success isn't taught in schools. It's all underground on apps and in YouTube videos. However, most people don't believe it will work for them, so when the video is telling people how to be, do, and have more, they think it's all done to make a quick buck. In reality, it sounds like the journey of 10,000 steps to the unknown. Much like saying, "easier said than done."

"Good luck with that" is what they might say or even "BS." When in reality, the amount of discipline required is not as much as people would think. Consistency and repetition are vital. Even if I said that the information in this book could increase your income ten times in less than two years, like it did for me, first, you would have to believe you can do it. And that will only work if you truly believe doing it will get you what you want.

That being said, unless you are willing to put in that time and effort, you won't want to hear the information this book has to give. To put it differently, there's an old saying: "The mind can only absorb what the seat of the pants can endure." If you don't want to do it, or don't believe you can, you're not going to do it no matter how much it works. Certainty, like clarity, trust, and flow, has a lot to do with people's actions. If you knew for sure, just by reading every word of this book, that within five years, you would make at least a million dollars a year, would you skip a word of this book?

The answer is and should be, "No." That's what faith and confidence, and many other principles from this book, will help you do. It will give you a sense of certainty to avoid feeling overwhelmed by the task in front of you. Because what I've learned over the last few years is that the keys to success are not the degree of the actions themselves, but the frequency of those actions, and as you know, it is all about what you can take.

There are a few habits that are impossible to do or take years of study before they can be tried. It's the basic, simple stuff that creates good habits in our life, removes bad ones, keeps us aligned with our goals and making progress, helps us avoid distractions, and so on and so forth.

Meet the "Now Client"

Up until now, we have answered the why, how, where, what, and when of real estate. This next part is about the *who*. In any business or industry, as the seasons change and the economic climate changes, the ideal client changes. In a market shift, if your business is suffering, don't change what you are doing because you just may be doing all the right things in front of the wrong people. The goal is to understand why markets shift and then you will know who the ideal client is for the new market.

The best way I know to describe why prices go up, shift, and then come down and keep repeating is to define what I call a "now client." These are prospects who are ready to buy or sell or do something real estate related. What you may already know is that a seller's market is when it's a good time to sell, and a buyer's market makes it a good time to buy.

If you are really good, you know that a seller's market is defined as zero-to-five months of inventory and a buyer's market is more than seven months of inventory. That information may help your score well on your real estate exam, but it is not going to help you before, after, or during a shift. However, knowing who your now client is and why they are your client will help!

When the market shifts, or things are bad and the economy is not as fruitful, people assume nobody is a now client. They think that everything is harder for everyone, prices are lower, but inventory is too high. They also assume that there are fewer people who want to do anything and that they're less qualified. Everything is harder. Even finding them, sifting through the competitive noise of other agents, and attracting attention to you specifically somehow seems harder to other agents. In reality, it's the exact opposite.

143

You know how they say, "When things get tough, the tough get going"? It's similar in real estate. When things get tough, people who have been living check-to-check or working part-time literally stop cold with their leads and don't get any transactions. Believe it or not, these people make up the majority of the real estate population. If you're not a full-time, active real estate agent, you are competing with a ton of agents just like you.

But those of us who've been at this for a year or two and want to do it as a career will already be in a position to not completely lose all your leads when the climate changes. It's a quicker shift than most people think. It could only be a couple of months before you get a new now client, (but for most) the gap is much larger. Just remember, if you can imagine your clients, you can attract them.

Regarding the now client in a seller's market, a seller's market begins when a buyer's market ends. Everything was on sale, and the prices were getting lower and lower. With prices being so low, everyone and their mother is ready, willing, and able to buy up all the inventory. That will spontaneously inspire more sellers to come out of the woodwork and start selling at the current fair market value, as more and more buyers take advantage of the discounts.

So right when a seller's market begins, your now client is actually a buyer. The beginning of a seller's market is the last chance a buyer has to buy before the prices start going up. Your now client is a buyer because they want to buy it all up while the prices are low. As they do that, the prices keep going up. Eventually, your now client becomes a seller who wants to keep selling and get the most money they can.

Technically, in a true and confident seller's market, savvy sellers will want to wait. If they wait a year, they can get more money for their house. So, now look at what happens. In a seller's market, your now client cannot be stopped from listing their house. Buyers need to act now. Every day that they wait, the interest rate to borrow the money increases, and so does the price of the house as more people keep selling and going under contract. Supply and demand is shifting.

At the beginning of a seller's market, your first client who needs to buy is your buyer, right? Yes. That's the last chance since the buyer's market just ended. Then, right away, your now client is the seller. The sellers can start selling if they have to, but some may wait. Because of that, your true now client is your buyer. It will now cost that buyer more money the longer they wait, period.

Now, as we're shifting from a seller's market back to a buyer's market, who's the very first client you're going to want to contact? A seller. It's their last chance to sell before they have to hold onto their house for two or three years. Historically speaking, a seller's market usually lasts longer than a buyer's market (also known as a correction) shortening the opportunity to buy.

Let's say you've lived in your house for almost a decade. You've just had your second child and need more room. You don't need to move immediately, but you'd like to move in a year or two. There's no hurry, but you see the market shifting, and you'd rather not wait five years to move. So you should definitely sell now. You are a now client.

Even though we're going into a buyer's market, every day you wait to sell your house at the beginning of this cycle reduces the amount of money you get for it. So, you need to sell your house fast. Even if you can't get as much as you want, the longer you wait, the less you'll get. Your buyers are then going to wait like the sellers do at the beginning of the seller's market. Every day they hold off, there's a fear that the market will fall even lower. Slowly but surely, buyers prepare to get a piece of the proverbial real estate pie and start buying again.

Know Your Client

Just remember that the true squeeze of any market shift is short-lived. It's usually only a month or two. It's not the end of the world. That is from a realtor's point of view, but to an investor, they may feel the effects of a down market much longer. Most investors know that you make your money when you buy not when you sell. The deals are during the buyer's market, which makes up a small portion of the market as a whole over time. By following the first sixteen chapters of this book, you're building professional relationships. You're influencing what other people do, helping them. You're not just advertising to random buyers and sellers. This way, you'll be fully equipped to keep those leads coming and going in your business during those market shifts. Then you'll know exactly who to center your advertising around. Based on the market itself, you'll be able to identify your ideal client. Knowing who that is, your industry, and yourself—and the services that you have to offer—is the recipe for success.

You must know your client. Based on the market, what are the goals of the majority of clients who are making transactions in this climate? Now, do you know who your now clients are and that they exist in any market?

The last piece of the puzzle is how and why the markets shift in first place. It comes down to supply and demand. However, there is often noise being made by doomsday predictors or people who are pessimists about anything. Truth be told, there is a fundamental truth about how we as people buy and sell things on the open market.

Imagine you are taking an important test with a group of fifty people, and five of you forgot your pen (which is required to take the test). The instructors have three pens, but there are five of you. One person raises his or her hand to offer $1 as compensation for that pen. A second test taker raises his or her hand and offers $2 for the second pen. Now, the other three students have the greatest motivation to claim that last pen. The fastest student, or the one that offers the most money, will get the last pen. In this example, demand exceeds supply.

Now imagine another test. This time, two students brought pens for themselves, as well as many more to sell. That is because word got out about what happens when students forget their pens, but this time only one student forgot a pen this time. When that student stands up to ask for a pen, the one student says, "Yes, I do, and I will sell it to you for $3." But the other student has a lot of pens, too, so he stands up and says, "I'll sell you one for only $2." At this point, the instructor steps in. "It is your lucky day; I have one extra pen and I will sell it to you for $1." Needless to say, that one student got to take his or her test and only spent $1 on the pen. Same pen, same class, same problem, but the outcome was completely different, and for a good reason—a principle, in fact.

People say, "Oh, it's the government! It's this; it's that. It's corruption. It's inflation." No, it's us. It's just the ebb and flow of human nature. The buyers will always compete with the sellers. We're nothing more than a society filled with consumers and producers. The ebb and flow of that value is what causes the market to fluctuate. It has done that before; it will do it again. You don't need to be afraid of it. You just need to identify it.

Are YOU Ready to Upgrade?

This idea dawned on me the other day while I was at the cellphone store with my daughter. She's never had a real phone before, and all she could focus on was the iPhone XS Max, which, if you know anything about current phones, is top of the line. My daughter is only eleven.

You can understand my confusion when she was asking for such an elaborate, expensive phone that is infinitely more powerful than the computers used to land the Apollo spaceship on the moon to play music and games. But she said something that made me think. After she asked if, when she gets straight As, if she could get that, and I asked her why she wanted to have *that* phone and not a less powerful one. Her reasoning was, "Well, it's the best, and I've got to have the best and the most updated. If I don't, in six months, the phone will be worthless anyway and I'll have to upgrade."

I thought to myself, "She's actually right." Maybe she doesn't need to have the best, and she's only eleven, but technology becomes quickly obsolete with each passing day. Along with that, every passing day after the release of the latest iPhone, Apple works day and night with the sole purpose of creating a better phone to do more and be more to us, and in exchange they can have more.

But do we upgrade ourselves as people? Has that thought ever entered your mind? After college, or halfway through a career, are you doing anything to enhance or upgrade your software, your mind? Are you introducing information into your brain that can help you process new information? Information that is changing and evolving every day.

Or are you walking around like an iPhone 3 instead of an iPhone 10X? So, I'm thinking to myself, as a person out of school, that it's easy to get caught up in the mundane tasks of life and not progress. We don't learn new things. We don't make ourselves better, more influential, impactful, nor knowledgeable. We wonder why we lose value. We wonder why we go through slumps.

See, time stops for no one. You are either moving forward or you're falling behind. If we're not learning new things, or at least more than the next person, we're at a huge disadvantage. All anyone has is twenty-four hours in a day and their God-given abilities. So, if we can maximize that—if we can use our minutes and seconds more effectively than anyone else, and do it for a greater amount of time, then we can be, do, and have anything we want.

You must understand that all these great, successful people that we see in the world are not some miraculous, divine human beings with powers that we'll never have. They either taught themselves, or they were born with a personality that allowed them to find the answers to these types of questions and gain an advantage to attain their goals.

I personally had to do it the hard way. I had to program everything that's in this book manually. I was not born this way. In fact, I was the opposite. I'm the free bird, easy-come, easy-go, no-big-deal kind of person. I didn't have the structure required for exponential growth, but I do now. Some people take the elevator to the top, and others take the stairs.

The reticular activating system in your brain, and the one in my brain, is what allows us to do that. We can reprogram ourselves and learn, do, and think differently whenever we want, for any reason. Our brains are more powerful than we will ever realize. Challenge it, and truly learn something new and important every day, and in time you will be amazed at what you are capable of.

There's No Stopping You!

The key to making this work long-term is committing to the daily morning activities. Every morning, you must commit to the mundane tasks using S.A.V.E.R.S. (the acronym to remember your tasks). On top of that, you need to make sure that you're aware of the obstacles in front of you and what can throw you off track. If you're not aware of them, they *will* overcome you and throw you off course.

Be aware of the voices in your head telling you not to do your runs, or your exercise, readings, or any of your morning activities. Aside from the weekends and emergencies—or if you're simply not home—there is no excuse for not continuing. Other than that, you have to do your S.A.V.E.R.S. every single morning, Monday through Friday.

These activities will be easy and the effects will be subtle. Nothing you receive from those activities will happen instantly. It's delayed gratification; it's the Brussels sprouts, not the candy. The good news is that they're as easy to do as *not* to do. There's no need to practice, but you need to be aware of your obstacles, that your body is going to try and break itself down. You might get really sick. You might injure yourself, and it's all going to happen because your subconscious is fighting the change. It's fighting the steps that are out-of-the-ordinary.

But you have to keep persevering by adding disciplinary actions so you'll stay on course. The key is to remember and commit, so no matter what, nothing will stop you from doing your daily activities.

Your First Three Steps

The first step involves analyzing yourself. Figure out what you want, what you are willing to do to get it, why you want to do it, and conclude the analyzation with a general breakdown of your typical workday from the time you wake up till the time you go to bed. In order to have or do anything we want, we must first *be* the person necessary to succeed. Analyzing your day allows you to see what you are doing that is not effective and replacing this with things that are.

The next step is your morning ritual, which includes waking up early and beginning your S.A.V.E.R.S., as well as a book list. The first book to read is *The Go-Giver* by Bob Burg and John David Mann. Next, start your morning rituals after you've read the book *The Miracle Morning* by Hal Elrod. In this book, S.A.V.E.R.S. has a special meaning that will explain what some of the other morning rituals are. It is important to familiarize yourself with many of these morning tasks. You might find them easy to do or easy not to do. They also have no timeline, and no one around you will be affected whether you do them or not. However, committing to them every day over a long period of time will guide you toward your goal and through any obstacle.

The third thing you're going to need to do is to look at your entire database—on your phone, mail, and client management system (CMS). Whether that is a list of past clients, friends or family, or just people you've met with a need that you want to help, you're going to use those names to find potential clients. Finding what those professional, business clients need and delivering the solution is the beginning of the process. The solution may have nothing to do with what you do, but it has everything to do with what they do, and what they need. I call that Influence. In *The Go-Giver*, the Law of Influence states that "Your influence is determined by how abundantly you place other people's interest first." You may not be paid directly for your advice, assistance, support, professional resources, or the general wisdom that you impart to that person, but if and when they return the favor, it will support what you get paid to do for a living.

To simplify it even further: What do you think is the best way to receive business or referrals? The answer is to *give* business or referrals. Sometimes, even the massive amount of people in a networking or referral group may not fully grasp the power of giving referrals. It may seem easier to do something nice, or say something helpful, to get something from someone else, but in the end, nothing is more effective than giving a referral. For that reason alone, it is vital that you find one or more social groups, clubs, and/or networking organizations that put you in a better position to give and receive referrals more abundantly to all.

Networking groups also grant more ownership of those established professional relationships, which happens to be more valuable and effective than even money. Loyalty in this setting is based on future and repetitive referrals. Therefore, the person doing the work is motivated by much more than what they will make on that deal. That translates to better workmanship and service to your client, a faster response to both you and the client, and what will most likely be at a lower or better price than a random vendor or service provider.

To summarize, this journey begins by removing your doubts and finding the answers to your questions. The first task is to find your "why" and own who you are. You must then create consistent morning rituals that will form consistent habits. These will lead to a positive mindset and positive results in your life. Your daily tasks and what you must do to stay productive in your career are also important, but not as important as the first two steps. Lastly, you have to focus on the client or your database of people who trust you to serve and help them.

Never cold call again, knock on a stranger's door, or make empty promises to your clients. You now know that a sales pitch ends with you asking for business. However, when you serve others in a way that is important to them, give them clarity on the process, and they trust that you are capable of doing the job, they will be *asking* you to work for them!

It is also important that you try not to overthink this and get caught up only reading and learning. *Done* is always better than perfect, and there is no better way to learn than by practice and preparation. As the Greek poet

Archilochus said, "We don't rise to the level of our expectations, we fall to the level of our training."

You may believe that you are not ready. No one is ever truly ready. You may think you don't have what it takes, but I am here to tell you that you have all the ingredients you need to succeed. You don't need money, fancy closing scripts, or years of schooling and experience. What really matters in the end is how we treat ourselves and others, and we can do that right now. The choice to do something is simply that, a choice. Therefore, success is not based on what we are *ready* to do but what we are *willing* to do. Choose wisely.

God Bless!

ABOUT THE AUTHOR

The first thing to know about Robert is that he prefers to be called Bobby. In fact when he meets clients for the first time, he introduces himself as Robert if he has never met them before. Knowing he is a relationship professional and that those closest to him refer to him as Bobby, his goal with each client is that they meet him as Robert, but by the end of the transaction and going forward, they would refer to him as Bobby. It is a fun way to make sure that the connection is strong and authentic. Robert may be his  birth name, but Bobby creates a whole new meaning when it comes to the quality of relationships he gains from all of his clients.

Bobby Paolini's tag line is "Licensed to sell, born to care, and ready to serve". Bobby's philosophy of creating a client centric perspective that sets the stage for trust and as a result smooth and easy sales transactions has resulted in extraordinary sales achievement. He has been recognized as an award winning top sales producer within his Real Estate company from the very first year he was in that business.

In addition to his own sales, Bobby is a sales trainer, and quickly becoming a highly sought-after speaker for those wanting to dramatically improve their sales abilities and take their business to the next level.

Bobby's biggest goal in life is to share the key concepts and principles that can help anyone successfully build professional relationships, have anything desired in life, and perhaps most importantly, create inner peace and a rock-solid self-confidence.

Bobby is forty years old, and since 1992 has been developing a massive network of professional relationships and vendors within the Palm Harbor area of Pinellas County to better serve his clients. He has been married for almost fifteen years, and he and his wife Leika have three amazing children ages eleven, nine, and seven. Having married his high school sweetheart, it is easy to see the connection between Bobby's love for people and relationships. His loyalty to his clients and those that refer him much of his business can be seen in his amazing relationship with his wife and children.